last copy

Bud Zukow M.D., is Chief of Pediatrics at AMI Tarzana Medical Center in Tarzana, California, where he is also in private practice. He lectures widely throughout Southern California to parent groups and schools and, when his schedule permits, attends UCLA games of all varieties. He has three grown children and lives in Woodland Hills, California with his wife Rozzi.

Margaret O. Ryan is a free-lance writer and editor in Los Angeles, California. She is the collaborating author of *Trances People Live* and *Therapeutic Metaphors for Children and the Child Within.*

Parent Power by Dr. Bud Zukow reflects his almost thirty years of experience as a pediatrician. Clearly he has learned enormously in these years about parents and about their children. The content of this book will provide a welcome insight for parents, which will not only be helpful to their children, but also to parents themselves. To this end, he had the able assistance of Margaret Ryan. It is a pleasure and a privilege to recommend this very clear, thoughtful, and helpful book to parents.

Benjamin M. Kagan, M.D.
Professor Emeritus of Pediatrics, UCLA
Director Emeritus Department of Pediatrics, Cedars-Sinai Medical Center
Senior Consultant Pediatrics, CSMC

∞

The paper used in this publication meets the minimum requirements of American National Standard for Information Sciences—Permanence of Paper for Printed Library Materials, ANSI Z39.48-1984.

Parent Power

Preserving Your Identity
Through Realistic Parenting

Bud Zukow, M.D.

With

Margaret O. Ryan

THE
BRAMBLE
COMPANY
Connecticut

For information write to:
The Bramble Company, RFD 88 (Route 126),
Falls Village, Connecticut 06031

Library of Congress Cataloging-in-Publication Data

Zukow, Bud.
    Parent power : preserving your identity through realistic parenting
/ Bud Zukow with Margaret O. Ryan.
    p.   cm.
    ISBN 0-9626184-5-4 (paper) : $12.95
    1. Parenting—United States. I. Ryan, Margaret O. (Margaret
O'Loghlin) II. Title.
HQ755.8.Z85   1992   92-12853
649'.1—dc20   CIP

First Printing 1992
1 3 5 7 9 10 8 6 4 2

Printed in the United States of America

With deep gratitude and affection
I dedicate this book

❧

To all the parents and children
I have worked with
in the past 28 years—
you have been my teachers. . .

To my own children,
Philip, Carlos, and Karyn —
you have shown me
what is really important in life. . .

To Rozzi, my wife and best friend,
for your patience, support, and endless humor...

And thanks to Margaret O. Ryan
for sharing five years of laughs and tears
and exciting moments that made this possible.

❧

Illustrations by Claudia Gray and Charlene Sieg
Cover photography by Bud Zukow
Cover photo: Ian Kaneshiro, 4 months

Contents ❧

Preface 🌿

There are plenty of books about childrearing that can tell you all the different ways you can give your baby...your toddler...your adolescent...your teen *everything* he or she could ever need emotionally and psychologically. You don't need one more "expert" telling you how to give *more* of yourself.

What you probably do need is some prodding to stop long enough to take a look at your lives as individuals and as partners, *apart* from your role as parents. You might be shocked by what you find. As a pediatrician and a father, I have spent several decades watching wives and husbands cope with parenting. In my 28 years of practice, I don't think I've seen one mother who was not abused by her parenting role for a significant period of time.

That is why I am also a *parent advocate*—which means that I'm on *your* side. Parent's rights as people are abused by their own misguidance, misgivings, and misunderstandings—*and* by a culture that idealizes and romanticizes the parenting role. Parents are misled into believing that raising children is like a scintillating trip through Alice's Wonderland. WRONG. It is more like riding a continuous roller coaster—one that sometimes comes to a stop for rest and refueling, but is mostly on the go, soaring high and swooping low.

Raising children may seem like a relatively minor challenge next to the crises that face us in the world today: rampant child abuse, the spread of AIDS, the growing number of homeless, the chronically ill, the stock market crash, world-wide terrorism, and on and on. But it isn't. On a personal scale, parenting can rank right up there with the worst of experiences. Life-threatening eating disorders, widespread substance abuse, teen pregnancies, and high school illiteracy are telling us, among other things, that we still have a lot to learn.

In talking to parents about childrearing issues, I am not trying to practice psychology. I do something else; *pediatricians* do something else. We observe and participate in the development of thousands of kids, and in the course of that involvement, we are brought into many other dimensions of family life. For this reason I believe that there is no one better qualified to discuss childrearing issues than the pediatrician. The pediatrician has the most contact with the entire family on an ongoing basis. I probably have four to eight conversations a day with parents about discipline, sleep problems, and eating disturbances.

Psychologists and mental health care professionals work with *pathology*. By the time they see the children, the family is usually in serious trouble. The books written by psychologists and psychiatrists about how to raise children are usually filled with a vast array of theories, concepts, and techniques espousing how to deal with or avoid pathology.

The pediatrician, on the other hand, is not trained in concept and theory. The pediatrician is trained to diagnose X and treat X *that day*. This is why, when a parent is having a discipline problem with a child, it is not important to me whether the child was breastfed; it's not important whether the mother was breastfed. What *is* important is that the child is getting out of control—

which is equal to X—and we are going to look for ways to solve X *that day*.

This is goal of my book: to provide a straight line from *problem* to *resolution*, uncluttered by theories, jargon, and unrealistic expectations.

When I began writing this book, I took a suspicious look at the prospect of putting myself in the position of giving "advice." I don't believe in advice. If there was one expert, one person with all the answers, then there would only be one book on childrearing in the bookstores. There would be no need for Dr. Spock or Dr. Mom or Dr. Brazelton or Dr. Bettelheim, or anyone other than *"The Expert."* Fortunately for all of us, there can't be one set of rules. If I were to measure my success by any kind of standard, I would measure it by the ability to help parents find their own standards.

We are not born parents, nor is parenthood the end result of giving birth. Being a parent involves the unfolding of experiences shared between parent and child on a daily basis, subject to change, rumbles, explosions, and storms of all kinds between each sunrise and sunset.

Good parenting, effective parenting, is not possible unless you are interested in your own growth as a person. When you lose sight of that, you step into the quicksand of the consuming/consumed cycle of parent enslavement. Your child becomes an extension of your own identity and the enmeshment—the enslavement—begins.

There is one central fact above all others that makes today's parents a special and unique breed: in many cases, we have had our children *by choice*. But if this heady realization leads to unrealistic expectations for what those children can and should become, we court disaster. For us as parents it can be difficult and painful to understand the highs and lows that accompany the changes in our children. The speed with which we are asked to comprehend and accept these transformations is sometimes mind-boggling. It is easy to fall into the trap of viewing every stage of the child's development (and of our own development as parents) as our *last chance* to make it better. What is worse, many of us already feel defeated and believe it is too late. A tunnel vision of unrealistic expectations causes us to isolate problems as if they were tragedies instead of seeing them as they really are—just *bona fide* slices of life.

I hope to show you how *not* to fight against normal problems as if they were a hallmark of your inadequacy, but instead to trust them and learn from them, creating a bridge of understanding from one stage of development to the next. I hope to show you how much you already know, how much of that is disregarded for various reasons, and how to re-establish the parameters you know will be best for you and your child.

1 ❦

What About Me?

Being a victim of parent enslavement means indulging your child's needs and demands while abandoning most or all of your own needs.

- Does it bother you that you haven't slept later than 6:30 a.m. since the baby was born three years ago?

- Does it bother you when you stop having sex to get milk, juice, or cookies for your midnight marauder?

- Does it bother you that a very little person seems to be constantly telling you *what* to do, *when* to do it, and *how* to do it?

- Does it bother you that your relationship with your spouse or partner always plays second fiddle to your child's needs and wishes?

- Do you frequently fall exhausted into your chair, imploring to yourself, *"What about Me?"*

If you find yourself answering *yes* to any of these questions, you may be a victim of what I call *parent enslavement*. Simply put, parent enslavement is what happens when children gain control of their parents and the household through the chronic use of manipulative behavior. In my 28 years of practice as a pediatrician, I don't think I've seen one mother escape this enslavement. (Fathers stand a better chance because they are generally around less.)

Parent enslavement is not some rare, bizarre crime that happens only in destitute families. It is something that happens *automatically* when you begin parenting. Parent enslavement exists for the majority of parents in one way or another. It exists all across the country, in high, medium, and low income families; in blue collar, white collar, and rural. At best, parents suffering from enslavement end each day feeling exhausted and drained. At worst, they teeter on the edge of desperation, as they fight to maintain some semblance of control over the children and themselves.

Parent enslavement begins the first time the parent has gone without sleep. If that is the second night the baby is home, or the second week, or the third month (excluding illnesses, of course), then that is when the enslavement begins. During infancy the parent has one foot in parenting and one foot in enslavement. But by the time the child is three, he or she has become an adept manipulator and the parent has moved into full-time slavery. There is that first trip to the market when your 2½-year-old asks for a piece of gum and you give it to him to keep his hands off the merchandise. A few months down the road you have reached the point of *asking* the child if it's okay to go to market. He says, "Only if I can have...", you give him what he asks for, and bingo, you're now more a slave than a parent.

I have listened to countless mothers as they sit across

from me looking haggard, frustrated, and even desperate. Their stories all have one common thread. They have lost control over their child, and they are afraid that re-asserting that control will mean that they are bad or abusive parents. Hence, the child reigns supreme while the parents frantically shadowbox with one another over *what to do!*

Let's finally blow open the silent conspiracy that surrounds parenting. This is a conspiracy that creates the Great Myth of Parental Fulfillment. It is the conspiracy that minimizes the difficulties and hardships and maximizes the joys and rewards. Joys and rewards are not what need to be emphasized—where is the problem in a reward? What parents really need to know ahead of time is the scope of the job they are undertaking. They need to be educated about what will be asked of them *every day* for the next 18 years (if you're lucky). I had one tired mother of a two-year-old tell me she felt *betrayed* because "nobody told me it would be nearly this hard!" First-time parents are usually fortified with nothing more than the fluff of illusions.

Was it like this for you? When you became pregnant, you were overjoyed. Creation is a thrilling process. As you look at the newborn there is the exclamation of joy and amazement, "Oh my God, look what we've done!" One year later you find yourself uttering the same words, "Oh my God, look what we've done," but in despair and disbelief that you are locked into this role forever.

The Great Myth of Parental Fulfillment is the foundation of parent enslavement. I see parent enslavement emerge in my parents out of simple naivete and unreal expectations. By not understanding what the crying means, what the tantrum means, what the testing means, parents fear the worst. If they better understood what to expect from the baby—that it's okay for the baby not to sleep right after it nurses; that it's okay for the baby to spit up, to cry in the middle of the night, to be cranky— *then they wouldn't develop that tremendous addiction to being needed that creates parent enslavement.* When you have unreal expectations about the baby, about the toddler, about the child, you get enslaved. Period.

I am a parent advocate. This does not mean putting the parent's needs before the child, and it does not mean indulging the parent's inadequacies at the expense of the child. It means bringing the other half of the picture into focus—the parent's half—so that their needs can be addressed and their feelings expressed. *What I have to say about parent enslavement may be of more value in the prevention of child abuse than all the books on how to raise a child correctly.*

There are many degrees of child abuse. There is the person who was himself abused and now continues the cycle by hitting and beating his own child. Such a person obviously needs intensive psychological help. But there are many people out there who end up abusing their kids in subtle ways—emotional and psychological ways—simply because they have become exhausted and overwhelmed by the job of parenting. They are not monsters; they are normal human beings who have been pushed beyond their limits.

As parents, we have all found ourselves "on the edge" many times; and our children have felt it, too. In exploring this concept of parent enslavement, I want to emphasize that it is not something that *the child does to the parent* or *the parent does to the child.* It simply comes with the territory. Given that, can a mother grow in her own directions and also nurture her child? Can she answer the question, "What about me?", in a manner that makes her want to get up in the morning? I believe so, with the help of a large amount of common sense and a willingness to learn about the ingredients of parent enslavement.

Babies and children don't intend to enslave their parents—it's just *very easy to do*. Why? Because of five universal qualities that characterize infancy and childhood:

(1) the complete dependency of the child upon the parent;
(2) the child's naturally self-centered behavior;
(3) the child's constant growth and expansion;
(4) the child's never-ending drive to *test* you; and
(5) the child's "cuteness con."

These qualities sound innocent enough. Children are constantly growing, constantly pushing back their boundaries, and constantly testing each and every limit you set. They are entirely consumed by what *they* need and want. When was the last time you heard a four-year-old ask, "How's your day going, Mom?"

Not to mention how much is tolerated out of sheer cuteness. The "cuteness con" works us all over and increases the quotient of manipulative behavior a hundred-fold! How many eating problems are rooted in the embarrassing fact that the undesired behavior was initially reinforced by the parents because they thought it was cute the first time they saw it?

Being a healthy child means being dependent, self-centered, growing, adorable, and testy. *Being a healthy parent*, meanwhile, means being able to look at those five qualities, understand them, and *set limits in relation to them*. Being a victim of parent enslavement, by contrast, means indulging your child's needs and demands while abandoning most or all of your own needs.

Abandoning most or all of your own needs happens more often than you might think. I have listened to countless stories in which parents naively describe a home life that amounts to concentration camp conditions. And guess who's in command?

In response to one mother's sobbing description of her weekend of manipulation, mayhem, and enslavement, I recalled a "Fairytale Nightmare" I had heard years ago.

Once upon a time, and that time was not in the past but in the future, a hard-working man and his equally hard-working wife were awakened by the sharp sting of a whip across their shoulders.

"Get up!" said a child's voice, "and wait on me!"

They opened their eyes in amazement and saw their child standing by their bed with a horse whip in his hand and scorn and fury in his eyes.

"Get up, I say!" the child repeated. "You," he barked, addressing the father. "Go earn money for me. And you," he added, addressing the mother, "Cook my breakfast and bring it to me in bed!"

Both obeyed without protest. Each realized with regret that by gratifying their child's every whim and permitting his increasingly unmanageable behavior, they had sowed the seeds of their virtual enslavement. They were now reaping the "crop" in the days, nights, weeks, months and years that they would remain as parents. They looked around and saw that in other homes the conditions were the same: fathers and mothers had become mere machines for grinding out pleasures and privileges for the child—none of which was good for *them*, the parents. *(Author unknown)*

F A I R Y T A L E   N I G H T M A R E

At first glance, the "Fairytale Nightmare" might strike you as an unlikely exaggeration. Yet I'm sure if you think of it the next time you are deluged by manipulative behavior, you will feel a somewhat disturbing resonance. The reality is, *children can and often do rule households.*

The Path of Best Intentions

The fact that parent enslavement is wrought out of the best of intentions was brought home to me by one mother's experience. By the time she came to me for a consultation, she and her husband were knee-deep in *living out* the Fairytale Nightmare. It was no exaggeration—the only thing missing was a clearly visible whip.

Rita had been stung from behind by the Great Myth of Parental Fulfillment. By trying to be the perfect mother, she had unwittingly given her child almost four years of training in how to dominate, manipulate, monopolize, terrorize, and enslave. Anna reigned as the center of their universe, which meant that Rita had lost control of her. In trying so hard to fulfill each and every one of Anna's needs, Rita had almost drowned in these needs. Now she sat before me with dark circles under her eyes, looking very beaten, and telling me that she was fighting depression every day. She had "no shred of self-esteem left," but didn't know what to do about it.

"Is this what good mothering feels like?" she asked, fighting back tears. "To turn myself inside out doing everything right and still come up *empty*? I'm so terrorized into believing that each and every move I make will have lifelong consequences—I end up feeling that an afternoon away from my daughter will haunt me the rest of my life."

"Rita," I said, "do you ever ask yourself, 'What about me?'"

"Well, sure, in a vague sort of way. I don't really think about it in so many words."

"Why not?"

"Because it seems selfish. Nothing's more important than Anna. It seems frivolous and self-indulgent to think about what I'd like to be doing. I just have to pull myself together—it's a matter of attitude."

"A matter of *attitude*?" I asked suspiciously.

"Yeah. You know, if I change my attitude and stop complaining, I'll feel better."

"Well, then you've come to the wrong place. I think your complaining is the one healthy thing I've heard so far. I won't help you change your attitude so that you can keep on mothering your life away. But I will help you change your methods of mothering so that there is something of yourself left over for *you*."

She looked at me as if I were speaking Chinese. "I thought I just needed to pull myself together."

"Pretty soon there won't be anything left of you to pull together."

"What do you mean?" By this time, her eyes were flooding with tears of recognition.

"I mean that the longer you ignore yourself by trying to be the perfect mother, the worse Anna's behavior will become, and the crazier you're going to feel. Do you *like* being brow-beaten by your four-year-old?"

"No! Of course not. But I don't know what to do about it. She's so used to getting her way. We're so used to *giving* her her way. The other night Jeff had just walked through the door, home from work. Before he or I could say two words, Anna was jumping up and down screaming, 'Daddy, talk to me—come to my room—talk to me…!' Jeff asked her in an imploring voice, 'Anna, honey, can I just have five minutes to talk to Mommy?' I listened to that quivering in his voice as he asked our four-year-old permission to talk to me and I realized we were in deep trouble. This isn't a once-in-a-while occurrence. It is actually very typical—our voices frequently quiver with uncertainty and anxiety."

"How long ago was that incident you just described?"

"Oh, about two months ago."

"What finally brought you in here today, two months later?"

"Anna's mouth! She criticizes everything I do—I'm intimidated by her! Yesterday I was playing with her in her room when I finally reached my breaking point. We were playing one of her favorite games where we make up stories with her toy animals and have them talk back and forth. Like I usually do, I let Anna have complete control over the direction our little drama was taking.

But the moment we began to play, Anna began to criticize. I chose the wrong pony, I said the wrong words, I moved the pony in the wrong way. I just went along, making the changes she demanded. Then, all of a sudden she dropped her pony, picked up a book, and sat down across the room to look at the pictures. Was I dismissed? No, indeed not! She also proceeded to tell me to continue playing our original game by myself. I was supposed to play both parts! [imitating Anna] 'Keep talking, Mommy, keep talking.'

"And I did, just like I had many times before—only this time I realized I felt foolish! And I felt like *I* was being punished. I told her I wouldn't continue to play the game by myself—she had to choose between the book and the game.

"She started to whine and nag that she wanted me to do it *her* way. In a burst of anger I screamed, 'No,' and stomped out of her room, slamming the door behind me. She came running after me and began shrieking— I mean, *really* shrieking—at the top of her lungs, 'I hate you! I hate you! I hate you!'

"That was it! Something in me snapped. I grabbed her and carried her, kicking and screaming, to her room. I came this close to hitting her—I *wanted* to hit her right then. Instead, I dropped her on her bed and slammed and locked her door. I had never *ever* used that lock on her door.

"Then I ran to my bedroom and fell apart. I cried so hard I couldn't even hear if Anna was screaming or crying in her room. I couldn't stop—I must have sobbed uncontrollably for a full hour.

"When I finally calmed down, I realized I—*we*— desperately needed outside help. That's when I phoned your office and made this appointment."

"Rita," I began, "in order to help you I have to be blunt. When you give Anna all that control, you're not being a parent. You're not even being a friend—I doubt that you would let a friend treat you that poorly. In kid's terms, Anna was 'mean' to you. In effect she said to you, 'You can't follow my instructions, so I'm going to do something else. For your punishment, you have to play both parts now.'

"Do you realize you were being abused?" I pressed. "That you were being a *slave*? From Anna's perspective, you were there to be manipulated by her, as she saw fit. And that is just what she did."

"It's hard to admit that things have come to that," Rita commented, softly.

"Well, it's not unusual," I assured her. "Do you know how many parents I see a week who are in the same boat as you? *Lots*. Over-parenting is rampant but it's not incurable!"

Rita finally laughed. "You mean there's *hope*?"

I told Rita to go home and, together with her husband, make up a list of the areas in which they felt a loss of control. What things hassled them the most? Then, she and Jeff could return for a consultation in which we would go over the list, prune it, and find ways to implement the most viable areas. (There is a more detailed example of this "Hassle List" in Chapter 4.)

Rita's fear was that taking care of some of her own needs would make her a selfish parent. It *is* really hard to be "selfish" as a parent. So many accusing voices hover in the rafters ready to criticize you. I tell my mothers that those voices will be there no matter what they do, so they may as well carve out some space for themselves, wrench their attention away from their kids, and start discovering who else besides a parent lives inside them.

In the following chapters, I hope to show you how to identify the things that *you* do that enslave you in your role as parent, and how to identify the things that *your child does* that cast you in your role as slave.

In the beginning, it may seem easier to simply get enslaved than it is to set limits and boundaries in the face of the most adorable creature in the world—your baby. In the long run, however, you will pay for your indulgence out of the sweat and sanity of your very being. If you sow the seeds of your own enslavement in those first years, you will indeed reap the grim results of what you sow—for the rest of your life.

The good news is that parent enslavement is curable! You can break into the cycle of your own enslavement at any point in time. Like Rita, you can work slowly and steadily to shift the foundation of your parenting methods. You can learn to set limits that work for you *and* your child....And then you can go about reaping the fruits of *those* seeds for the rest of your life!

2 ❦

The Consumed / Consuming Cycle

Children should not be consumed by their parents, and parents should not be consumed by their children. The first leads to a vicarious life lead through your child, and the second leads to a breakdown in discipline and loss of control.

When I visit a new mother in the hospital after her delivery, one of the things I tell her is to get a babysitter and go out to dinner with her husband the first weekend she and the baby are home. Why? Because if you don't start *letting go* from the beginning, the complete dependency of the infant becomes *the complete dependency of the parent*. As a parent, you *learn to need* to have your child dependent on you and, as a consequence, you fall into consuming and consumed behavior: You learn to *consume* and *to be consumed*. You develop the habit (and, perhaps, even the addiction) of tending to the child's needs 100 per cent of the time. *You become dependent on the dependency itself,* and that is what opens the door to being manipulated by the ever escalating scale of what the child wants and demands. Therein you become the victim of parent enslavement. Therein lies the collapse of your identity, your autonomy, and your daily sanity!

My philosophy for parenting in the nineties is simple: *Children should not be consumed by their parents, and parents should not be consumed by their children.* The first leads to a vicarious life lead through your child, and the second leads to a breakdown in discipline and, eventually, to a devastating loss of control. *Both* lead to your emotional enslavement.

When we talk about consuming behavior, we are talking about a *cycle* in which, truly, "what goes around, comes around." The consuming cycle begins with the arrival of the baby, which signals the new parent's instant transformation into a 24-hour-a-day caretaker. Suddenly the parent is at the beck and call of an infant every moment of the day and night. The helplessness and all-encompassing needs of the baby inexorably draws the unseasoned parent into *being consumed* by those needs.

Once this portion of the cycle is underway, it is not long before the parent *is doing the consuming*. Here is where the parent begins to actively participate and *even initiate* her or his enslavement. Here is where the complete dependency of the infant becomes the complete dependency of the parent.

The Parent Who Is Doing the Consuming

The parent who is doing the consuming becomes over-protective, smothering, and ever-present. She (or he) establishes a pattern of over-parenting that has at its core, a mode of constant *surveillance*: the parent never stops looking for something to correct, protect, fix, or direct. The parent who *is consuming* is the parent who does not allow the baby to fall down; does not allow the baby to feed itself for fear it won't get enough to eat; does not allow the child to make the choice of whether or not he/she needs a jacket.

The mother who is knee-deep in consuming behavior usually believes she is the only person who is qualified to act as a caretaker. Even the husband can become a casualty along the way. One mother told me:

> I remember the paranoia I went through when Lily was a baby. Lyle, my husband, would come home from work and be perfectly willing to dress her and take her in the stroller to the park. All of a sudden, I saw him as a total incompetent who didn't even know how to dress her. Worse, I started having horrible fears of her getting seriously injured at the park with Lyle, once I let go of her. I would almost wait for the phone call and could see myself in the emergency room. I became so obsessive that I sabotaged all sources of support for myself when it came near the area of caretaking for Lily. Fortunately, my husband has a strong sense of himself, so he was able to confront me. If he had simply put up with it, I doubt that our marriage would have survived Lily's third birthday.

Take another common example of the child who cries when leaving his mother to go to nursery school for the first time. Why is it that the mother has to interpret that crying to mean: "He wants to stay with me...I should keep him with me...he'll never get along without me...it's cruel of me to make him go."

None of these statements may be true. The child is simply saying, "I'm scared of new things." Who isn't? What adult doesn't get anxious about beginning a new job, or starting an educational program of some kind? When the child cries and the parent responds internally with, "I'm so needed...if I let him go he's not going to love me...he'll think I don't love him," that is the beginning of trouble. For when the parent indulges in those kind of ruminations that foster and reinforce the child's continued heavy dependency, *the parent is creating his/her own enslavement.*

THE CONSUMING PARENT

As a consuming parent, do you frequently find yourself in a surveillance mode?

You might ask, but doesn't the dependency automatically diminish as the child gets older? *NO.* The dependency diminishes *only when the parents let go.* And the *letting go* can begin on Day One. It doesn't mean you don't like being a parent; it doesn't mean you don't dearly love your child.

I have parents who are always on their child's case. They go through a whole production before they come for an office visit: the shower, the spotless clothes, the matching socks, the Sunday shoes. Those are all demands they put on the kids—and on *themselves*. I'm not suggesting that they bring their kids in dirty and slovenly, but I am suggesting that they loosen up, lighten up, and *let go*. When they ask me why their child is unhappy, I tell them bluntly it's because *they never want to stop parenting*. That pattern of watching over another human being and caretaking, and molding, and correcting, and directing—it's all *habit forming*, and it *is* very difficult to stop or diminish.

I had a surprising realization. I have never had a parent tell me that she thought her child was just fine when she brought him in for a check-up. Yet I have seen plenty of kids arrive for their check-up in robust health. There is that over-concern that seems to get imprinted in those first months of infancy—only now the child is five years old and hasn't had a sick day since his last ear infection over three years ago! There is no need for concern, yet concern and worry still grip the parent-child relationship.

The Parent Who is Being Consumed

The consuming parent invariably finds herself confronted by a consuming child. This is a child who has learned how to manipulate you with his behavior. This is the child who has learned how to play you "like piano keys." One morning, the mother who has devoted every ounce of attention, energy, and strength to the caretaking of her child for the past 2½ years, suddenly realizes she is being worn ragged by the demands and manipulations of this little being. Yet she has been *so scrupulous* in nurturing. *Nurturing*?! Now she is begging, pleading, bribing, bargaining—anything to control the chaos of her rampaging toddler, her marauding pre-schooler.

In the beginning she as the parent did the consuming: she did the hovering, the obsessing, the fussing, the constant surveillance. Now, just to survive, she switches out of the surveillance mode and into a *defensive mode*:

How can I get the marketing done without going through eight temper tantrums or three boxes of cookies, whichever comes first?

How can I get 30 uninterrupted minutes of time to study for my one class?

How can I get my child to sit still and eat one meal without it ending up on the floor and the walls?

T H E   C O N S U M E D   P A R E N T

As a consumed parent, do you frequently find yourself in a defensive mode?

In essence, Mother has moved from the offensive position of *consuming* to the defensive position of *being consumed*. She is definitely no longer smothering her child with attention because that child is now chasing her down the football field, wielding all the power he has amassed in the last few years of being the sole center of her universe.

If you are being consumed by your child's demanding behavior, you obviously have done some consuming, or your child wouldn't be wielding that kind of power. If you haven't felt driven to parent 24 hours a day, it is unlikely that you'll find yourself confronted by a consuming three-year-old.

With my parents, I have found it is useful to help them identify where they are in the consuming cycle. It gives them perspective so that they are not at the mercy of the strong currents of the cycle. It also helps them make specific changes in their methods of parenting. Let's begin by answering basic questions that will help you locate your position within the consuming/consumed cycle.

Are You As the Parent Doing the Consuming?

As I have said, the parent who is doing the consuming is in the *surveillance mode*. She is the one who is initiating the focus and the attention on the child.

- Do you feel/believe that you are the only really competent caretaker for your child?
- Can you periodically let your four-year-old dress herself and not change her clothes after?
- Can you let your child make a decision about needing or not needing a jacket?
- Can you let your child (even your infant) decide to eat or not eat?
- Can you let your child decide to sleep or not sleep?
- Are you constantly comparing your child to your friend's children?

- Do you find that every moment of your day revolves around the needs of the baby, without a thought to yourself?
- Do you spend most of your time with the baby, and almost none with another adult? Then, when you are with an adult, do you find that your conversation is monopolized by the subject of your baby?

A PARENT WHO IS DOING THE CONSUMING
IS A PARENT WHO IS BECOMING ENSLAVED

Are You As the Parent Being Consumed?

The parent who is being consumed is in the *defensive mode*. She is being constantly dragged into involvement with the child via manipulative behavior.

- Does your child tell you what to do, when to do it, and how to do it?
- Do you have to bribe your child throughout the day in order to accomplish your various tasks?
- Do you stop having sex to get milk, juice or cookies for your marauding midnight toddler?
- Do you have to run to the bathroom and lock the door so that you can have a few moments of privacy?
- Do you ask your three-year-old for permission to talk to "Daddy" first?
- Do you find yourself intimidated by your four-year-old's bad-mouthing?
- Do you frequently go to bed at night feeling that the household is out of control?

A PARENT WHO IS BEING CONSUMED
IS A PARENT WHO IS BECOMING ENSLAVED

If you've answered yes to either set of questions, take heart. The remaining chapters of this book will give you very practical ways to interrupt the consuming/consumed cycle in relation to all the major issues of childhood: sleeping and eating problems, discipline, school problems, and so forth.

Consumed by Experts

Experts help foster the consuming cycle and create the inevitable enslavement of it by telling parents, for example, that if their baby doesn't sleep through the night, they should hold her all night long if necessary. They help create enslavement by romanticizing bonding as a blissful state of inseparableness between mother (or madonna) and child. Never being separated from your baby is *not* blissful. It is *stressful, straining, exhausting*, and even *crazy-making*.

Similarly, breastfeeding your child for two or three years is not necessarily a cherished experience of bonding, as some experts croon. It can end up being a literal experience of enslavement. Far from bonding the child to you in a loving, reciprocal manner, it ultimately places the child in a position of power and dominion over you.

I had one mother come to me for the first time when her child was almost five years old. To my horror, she told me she was still breastfeeding! She also told me that she and her husband had not spent one night alone in their bed since this child's birth. Not only did their child not sleep through the night yet—she didn't even sleep in her own bed!

The mother was surprised at my shocked reaction. Hadn't I heard of the concept of the "family bed" in which the experts tell you that it's fine for parents and children to share a bed, just like in colonial times? I had heard of the family bed but, frankly, the idea of it outraged me. Often, the marital bed is *the* only remaining sanctuary for new parents—the one place where they can hope to focus on one another. To open this last vestige of privacy to the domain of the child is, in my view, to invite disaster in the marriage.

I felt my usual stabs of anger and sadness as I looked

at this mother whose face looked 44 instead of 24. Both she and her husband were in bondage, but they were unable to recognize it and call it by name. They, like thousands of other parents, believed that to raise a healthy kid, you had to bond to it like epoxy glue. Having done that, they then wondered why they felt like they were jumping out of their skin.

The mother told me she was a "nervous wreck" and asked if I would prescribe a tranquilizer. I told her the only tranquilizer she needed could be gotten without medication when she weaned her child. She knew it was time to stop breastfeeding, she said, but she couldn't face the wild battles of will that weaning would trigger. I gave her the "Hassle List" assignment and the name of a family therapist I respected and told her to make an immediate appointment.

This mother came into my office defending her five years of breastfeeding and denying that was the problem, yet telling me she was on the verge of a nervous breakdown. She left my office visibly relieved, having finally been able to say that *she* wanted to stop breastfeeding, and that she and her husband desperately needed time away from their child. She was ready and willing to change her consuming behavior. All she needed was some well-placed guidance and help in breaking her long-established patterns of enslavement.

Some people, however, *like* the enslavement and don't want to hear one single word about how they should take time away from their kids. If you're comfortable being a slave to your kids, then you haven't got any problems and you don't need to read this book. More often than not, however, one parent *will* have a problem with it.

One day I got a phone call from one of my fathers.

"I'm desperate—I need help," he said with embarrassment. "My wife absolutely won't go anywhere without the kids and it's driving me crazy."

I wasn't surprised. They had four-year-old twins and a 15-month-old toddler. The mother had had tremendous difficulty separating from the twins, and now she was re-engulfed in the youngest. I gave the father the phone number of a psychologist.

About ten days later the wife came in and I casually asked, "Patti, how's Leonard?"

"Awful," she answered.

"Why?"

"Oh, the usual. He's not going to feel better until I go away with him without the kids—and I'm not going to do that!" Her sister, who also refuses to leave her kids for a second, was with her. They giggled like two school girls with a secret.

"You know," I began tentatively. "Perhaps the only reason you don't want to go away without your children is because you don't want to be alone with your husband and you don't know how to say so." They giggled again, completely oblivious to how serious I was in my statement.

Parent enslavement doesn't upset me if both parents are comfortable living their lives for their kids. It only upsets me when I begin to see pain, fatigue, and turmoil surround one or both parents. I take that as a signal to intervene, and I intervene by helping the parents identify their patterns of consuming behavior.

If you have an upset stomach and you take something for it, it goes away and you feel better. If you eat the same food three days later that upset your stomach before, you'll feel sick again—which means that you are not learning. This is what happens with us as parents. Indoctrinated by the Great Myth of Parental Fulfillment, we keep doing the same things over and over again that perpetuate our own enslavement. We keep consuming and being consumed by giving in to manipulative behavior and by indulging our own needs to control, parent, and smother.

By reading this chapter and locating yourself in the consuming/consumed cycle, you have taken the first step toward your own liberation. This is a liberation that also frees your children to grow in their own directions—to start becoming considerate, responsive human beings with their own goals, desires, and dreams. *That* is liberating.

3 ❧

We Are Not Born Parents

I have yet to encounter a perfect parent. But I have encountered countless sets of parents who were temporarily trapped in the mire of trying to be perfect. With each office visit I see the parent fade further and further away as a person...When you stop being a person to become a caretaker, it feels like you have lost the right to your own set of needs.

The myths and unreal expectations surrounding parenting lay the foundation for the consuming/consumed cycle that is the core of parent enslavement. We are not born parents, but we are expected to parent as if we were. Becoming a parent is a little like opening up a complicated toy from "Toys-R-Us" that comes with a *blank* sheet of instructions. You are expected to know what to do with this completely vulnerable, brand new human being, for whom you are totally responsible 24 hours a day. It feels like you just stepped into a Twilight Zone filled with foreign things like diapers, schedules, baby spit, and crying sounds.

There is a silent conspiracy of unrealism that surrounds our culture's view of parenting. It is a conspiracy that denies the difficulties and hardships and maximizes the joys and rewards. Life, in this view, is like a Clairol ad where mother and daughter float across a beautiful field of flowers on a sun-glorious day. In reality, there is a painful gap between what new parents expect of parenthood and what they discover it to be. This gap has many sources of input, all of which concern me because of the net outcome: parents in pain because they think they don't know how to parent.

The mother who collapses in exhaustion at eleven o'clock at night wondering, "How can I do this for another 18 years?" is in a great deal of pain. The father who berates himself because he doesn't have time to take his four-month-old to the gym for "Toddler's Gymboree" three times a week is in pain.

I think it is time we begin speaking with more honesty about the *parent's side* of the child-parent equation. It is time to say openly that raising a child not only gives you a great deal, it also *takes something from you.* Parenting takes countless hours of time, selfless effort, and work —and parents need to learn how to cope with these all-consuming demands.

When parents feel ineffective, they will inevitably parent ineffectively. To function effectively, parents need *realistic* information about the scope of the job they have undertaken. Yet they are usually fortified with nothing more than the fluff of illusions handed them culturally as well as commercially. I've had many tired mothers tell me they feel "betrayed" because "nobody told me it would be nearly this hard!" The next sentence is invariably the one the causes the most harm: "I must be doing something wrong." A verdict of "guilty" and "incompetent" breeds within most mothers at one point or another during their early parenting years.

Most parents either vividly remember or vividly repress their earliest experiences with their newborn. One mother described her fiasco: "I practically ripped off my baby's three-hour-old skin! The nurses brought her to me in a bassinet and said, 'Here's your baby.' Well, she pooped in her diaper the second she looked at me, and so I had to change her with my mother hovering over me and my husband flying around the room with a zoom lens. I didn't know the little trick of folding the tape over before pulling if off—and I certainly didn't think of it at that point. The tape stuck to her skin; I yanked it but it wouldn't budge—so I just yanked a little harder! My mother was horrified."

My mother's favorite story was the time she waited four hours for me to put my arm in the sleeve of a shirt— and I was five days old! She honestly thought that I would move my arm into the sleeve of my own accord, and that I must be defective if I didn't. When my father came home from work, my mother was in tears, I was sound asleep in her arms, and she was still waiting for me to move my arm!

These stories are lighthearted examples of the gap that exists between what new parents expect parent-hood to be, and what they actually encounter in their day-to-day living of it. I have many stories that are not so lighthearted. I have found that most of us begin parenting completely unaware of the assumptions, ex-pectations, and values that are driving us. This unawareness functions a little like a trap into which the parent falls in her or his most vulnerable moments. It is a trap that ensnares the parent in a consuming cycle of ineffective parenting and self-condemnation.

That is why I feel the first step in avoiding or undoing the consuming/consumed cycle is to bring these hidden variables out into the open. Toward that end, we are going to take a look at several myths I have found to be the most harmful to parents' sense of self:

The Myth of the Perfect Parent

The Myth of the Experts

The Myth That "Parenthood Won't Change Our Relationship"

The Myth That to Know Your Baby Is to Love Your Baby

In each of these categories ask yourself, *What are my assumptions about being a parent? What are my expectations and values?* Then ask, *Are they helping me or harming me?* Take a close, honest look at how these myths affect your daily experience of being a parent and your own evaluation of yourself as a parent. At the end of the chapter, take some time and fill out the checklist entitled, "Checking Your Myths at the Door."

The Myth of the Perfect Parent

Most of us struggle heroically to be the "perfect parent." Perfect parents have *no* personal needs or imperfections to speak of. Perfect parents never feel like jumping out the window, locking themselves in the bathroom, or sending the kid to camp for 12 months. Perfect parents never find themselves *praying* for an uninterrupted orgasm. Instead, the perfect parent is someone like Dr. Mom—a SuperPerson who can nurse five babies, rock them devotedly through their all-night crying jags, and all the while attend medical school full-time!

28

In my decades of interacting with hundreds of families, I have yet to encounter anyone who was a perfect parent. But I have encountered countless sets of parents who were temporarily trapped in the mire of trying to *be* perfect. The result? With each office visit I see the parent fade further and further away as a person, only to be replaced by an increasingly frazzled and frantic *caretaker*. When you stop being a person to become a caretaker, it feels like you have lost the right to your own set of needs. No more nail appointments; no more shopping trips by yourself; no more languid library excursions.

Recently a mother asked me, "Is it okay if we go out for a ride?"

"Sure," I said.

"Well," she stammered, "we don't want to take the baby—she's only three weeks old."

"That's perfectly all right," I assured her. "You can go for a ride without the baby."

"What if we want to stop for ice cream and we're a little late getting back?" she asked timidly.

"That's okay, too," I answered casually.

Then came the point of the whole conversation. "You know," she began, "*my mother said* that we shouldn't leave the baby at all. She said it would hurt her to leave her with someone else."

All I could say was, "I don't believe that's true. I think your baby will be a lot better off if she has semi-sane parents around her 22 hours a day, and a babysitter for the remaining two!"

Trying to be the perfect parent inevitably ensures that you will get caught up in the consuming/consumed cycle. For this reason, I think it can be helpful to recognize on a feeling level that you are not born parents, and that you cannot be perfect at parenting.

Your Perfection Through Your Child's Eyes

It is not difficult to try with all your might to do your best for your child—but still mess him or her up at some point.

You can begin by telling your five-year-old, who has just toddled into the kitchen in the morning in his bare feet, "Go get your slippers on! You'll catch pneumonia!" Your parental concern will go right over his head, but he will get the message that he must be stupid to think his bare feet are comfortable. So he puts his slippers on, even if his feet aren't cold, and in the process becomes increasingly dependent on you, the parent, to know when *he* is comfortable. From this type of experience, the child learns to look to others to adjust his emotional and physical climate, and he begins to learn *not* to trust the validity of his own "thermostat."

Your child is now ready to sit down to a breakfast of hot oatmeal, soft-boiled egg, and fresh strawberries. You tell him that if he eats it all, he'll grow up to be big and strong. More conflict: if he eats it all, he'll vomit, but if he doesn't, he'll be a dwarf. More messages not to trust his inner barometers.

Halfway through the oatmeal, your child's gag reflex kicks in, and he is sent to his room until noon by a parent who is genuinely afraid that his eating habits will lead to illness or malnutrition.

At 11:30 a. m. you stomp into your child's room, demanding to know if he ate the chocolate candies in the refrigerator. While you are yelling, "Did you or didn't you?", your child is working the remaining chocolate off his chin with his tongue. He obeys a natural instinct to defend himself in the face of such adversity by lying. You become even angrier when confronted with this bold-faced lie and begin to lecture on the sin of lying.

Your child is beginning to feel like a ping-pong ball, bouncing back and forth between offenses. But he cannot "learn from the experience" because the experience has become too muddled. From the breakfast table, to the chocolate caper, to the lie—the day, so far, feels just plain crummy.

At noon you tell your child to get ready for his drum lessons. When he says he hates drum lessons and doesn't want to go, you remind him of the sacrifice being made to provide this private instruction. And what was the word you called him—an *ingrate*??—whatever that means.

Getting ready for the lesson, the child feels sluggish and nauseous. About the only things he's sure of at this point in the day are his inability to determine when he is or is not comfortable, and how much trouble he causes. He puts on his clothes and goes out to the garage to join you, but you are disconcerted by his overly short pants and the hole in his shirt. When your child begins whining that he feels comfortable in these clothes, you snap in frustration, "Don't be ridiculous!"

Now your child finds himself discarding his own choices in favor of something he is told is more appropriate. To his chagrin, he learns that just because something feels soft and good does not make it right. He is actually receiving expert training on how to ignore his own feelings. The seed of your idea that it is more important to look good than feel good has been firmly planted.

After the drum lesson, you take him to the soda fountain. The pleasure of the treat is displaced, however, by your distress over the dribbles of ice cream that have ended up on that expensive new shirt.

On the way home, your child whines and complains about the drum lesson while you wail in return, "What do you want from me!" When he answers, "All I want is a GTO skateboard," you feel like sending him to his room again.

Your *Imperfection* Through Your Own Eyes

From your perspective, the day has been just as harrowing for you. From morning till night, you are in conflict over when to discipline, when to nurture, and when to simply butt out. It seems as if your child is always wanting to do the opposite of what is best for him. He eats only what he feels like eating; he wears only what is raggy and comfortable; he walks around barefoot every chance he gets; and he stubbornly refuses to take advantage of the opportunities you work so hard to make available to him.

On one hand you realize that he is only a child and should be allowed a "child's play." But on the other hand, you feel committed to raising your child with a good set of values and to give him every opportunity to realize his potentials. Somehow, these fine motivations inevitably translate into the most banal, aggravating daily routines of fighting and haggling over every little thing.

Where is the sense of achievement and gratification you had envisioned would go along with this sacred task of caring for another human life? How did the worthiness of parenting disintegrate into a morass of petty daily skirmishes?

Super Babies. . .But Still Imperfect Parents

The above scenario is a lightweight version of what Superbabies and Superparents experience in the course of one of their grueling days. As a pediatrician and as a father, I am frankly horrified by the Superbaby movement and believe that its very starting point is this illusion of being the perfect parent. There are actually two-year-olds out there currently attending school to the tune of $12,000 a year! I have a somewhat crass fantasy that the parents of these two-year-olds made their reservations for these schools before they even got out of their love-bed. The tender moment might go something like this:

"Are you done?"

"Yea, I'm done."

"Okay, let's call just in case!"

It is easy to make jokes about the superbaby movement because it is a caricature of what every one of us as a parent experiences: the burning desire to give our kids everything possible, and to have them turn out to be brilliant *and* attractive *and* emotionally adjusted *and* in a profession we happen to value highly. Paradoxically, I have seen so much harm come from this quite natural set of motivations, however, that I have forced myself and many of my parents to take a closer look at what breeds beneath their shining surface.

"Don't Be Who You Are —
Be Who I Think You Should Be"

The implicit but oh-so-loud-and-clear message given to the child of parents trying to be perfect is one of *"Don't be who you are—be who I think you should be."*

Don't be a quiet, low-key child who enjoys playing alone—get out there and make some friends, join some clubs, *participate.*

Or

Don't be so loud and noisy—be quiet and refined like your father.

Or

Be more athletic—it's good for you!

Or

Try harder—you'll never get ahead in life without pushing.

Or

Learn to play classical piano—you'll be glad later.

Or. . .Or. . .Or

This is a subtle type of abuse that infuses the households of would-be perfect parents. It is not a TERRIBLE physical or emotional abuse—the child is not getting beaten or locked in closets all day long. But there *is* an abuse of identity and of individuality: the child is robbed of the opportunity to develop as a separate human being. To be blunt, the parent is guilty of using the child to pad his or her own ego. We have all done it before, and we will probably all do it again. The lines of identity and individuality get very blurred and merged in the process of parenting children. But that doesn't mean we should hide it beneath sterling motivations that we are just trying to give our child everything. We are *also* trying to give ourselves everything.

We are all guilty of these attitudes at one point or another. The important point is to monitor how much and how often.

The "Better Than" Trap

The second implicit but loud message to the child of perfect parents is the continuous injunction to *be better* than every other little two-year-old or three-year-old. I have never seen achievement encouraged in a vacuum. It is *always* accompanied by a means of comparison and an object of competition, which is invariably another child or roomful of children.

I don't think *achievement* or *competition* has any formal place in a young child's life. Children will engage spontaneously in competitive activities with one another, and they will spontaneously strive to explore their own abilities and desires. In the superbaby environs, the two-year-old is being taught tremendous competitiveness; he or she is pressured into trying to be *better than* all the other little two-year-olds. In my experience, the "better than trap" nets few dividends and all kinds of unwanted outcomes—such as having the first two-year-old with a diagnosed ulcer.

By the age of two or three, many a preschooler is already in the uncomfortable position of being stringently evaluated. But does a two-year-old or a three-year-old or even a five-year-old *really* care where she lands in her preschool class? I don't think so. But her parents do, and her parents' feelings about how well or badly she is doing in preschool are going to effect how she feels about herself each and every day.

In the long run we have got to be brutally honest with ourselves when we look at our perfect-parent ideals and evaluate what toll these ideals are taking on our children—*and* ourselves—for, to the degree that we abuse and merge and blur our children's identities with our own, we abuse our own identities as well.

The Myth of the Experts

Is this a common if somewhat exaggerated scenario for you? Your five-year-old is eating chocolate 15 minutes before dinner. He feeds it to his baby sister, who vomits on the TV during the NFL game of the week. Meanwhile, you are trying to cook said dinner and talk to your mother on the phone at the same time.

At the sound of chaos erupting, you stop cooking and scream at your husband, "The book, the book! Give me the book that tells us what to do now!" You have already tried every trick you know in the course of your ten-hour day. Now, you need the experts. Your husband promptly brings you the book and you flip through the pages, coming to the ones that are dog-eared. Scanning down the page, you read the words:

> Speak in a very soft and steady voice. Say something to the effect of, "I see that something is bothering you. Are you angry? Mommy often feels that way too."

But as you gallantly try to execute this sage advice, you discover that your five-year-old has just torn up your entire stack of paid bills, tied his baby sister to the basement door, locked your husband in the bathroom, and started a small but effective fire in the living room! Don't look at the expert's book! Stop cooking. Stop arguing. After you've put out the fire and untied and unlocked everybody, go for a short walk. Ask yourself how a five-year-old child got hold of chocolate that you don't want him to eat in the first place. You bought it. Who has given him permission to "express himself" in almost any manner known to human or animal? You have. Who tells your mother to call anytime? You do. Who feels totally responsible for the well-being of the children and the upkeep of the house? You do. Realize how much of this chaos you actually have control over and can change. And realize how far your own intuition and common sense can go in finding solutions that make *you* feel better.

Ultimately, the only true experts in childrearing are parents themselves. Yet, the publishing industry is consistently deluged with books about childrearing by "experts."

As Edward Ziegler, psychologist at Yale University, expresses it: "The fact that the advice preferred in one decade is seldom consistent with that offered in the next has not diminished the popularity of expert advice on childrearing."

I know a real-life expert on childrearing, and it's not me. It's Leona O'Hare. She has six children (five girls, one boy) and 12 grandchildren, and I take care of all of them. My expertise lies in putting medicine together with kids' bodies and behavior. Her expertise lies in parenting effectively and lovingly while somehow still managing to maintain her own identity.

There are ample books available to tell you about everything the baby and child go through developmentally, and everything that you can do in order to respond lovingly and effectively. Childrearing books are undeniably geared toward what the *child* needs from the *parent*. But parents are still left in a vacuum when it comes to dealing with their own needs (physical, psychological, and emotional) as human beings. The emotional toll parents experience is rarely addressed in any realistic fashion.

How long can a mother stay loving when she does not have one minute entirely to herself in the course of her 14-hour day? How do parents deal with the guilt they feel when, after a week of listening to their baby's crying, they teeter on the edge of exhaustion and wonder, "How am I ever going to survive this?"

In my experience, what parents need more than anything in the world is a sense of confidence in their own abilities to parent effectively. This means learning to trust that their perceptions and responses are accurate and based in reality.

But you can't have clear perceptions and responses when you are operating on four hours of sleep a night, or when you are at the mercy of a ruthless two-year-old tyrant. In short, you can't have clear perceptions and responses when you are enslaved in your parenting role, catapulting back and forth in the consumed/consuming cycle.

"It Won't Change Our Relationship"

In one of my meetings with parents, I asked a group of 20 to discuss the commonly held myth that having a baby does not change the husband-wife relationship. For the next 30 minutes, lively discussion jumped back and forth from one participant to another—but not one of them talked about his or her spouse and how they related. Everyone talked about the kids! For most of us the unique interpersonal aspects of our man-woman relationship quickly vanish in the haze of parenting.

If, as a parent, you have ever entertained the wild illusion that your relationship with your spouse hasn't changed with the coming of the baby, just take a moment to recall the first time your toddler ever so innocently interrupted the first sex you had in three weeks by padding into your bedroom at two o'clock in the morning to check out the noises he was hearing or beg for a glass of milk? It leaves you wondering if climax will ever be the same! The bare reality is that every facet of your husband-wife relationship changes with the birth of your first baby. Indeed, many facets of your individual identities also undergo significant alterations. As a wife, you are no longer primarily a woman and a professional partner; now you are a Mother (capitalized) with only mild hopes of someday being at least a part-time breadwinner again. As a husband, you are no longer primarily a courting male and a breadwinner; now you are the primary Breadwinner (capitalized) and reigning Father Figure.

One mother put it this way: "Mothers who stay home with their babies go through *withdrawal* because they're not going to work everyday. When I first got home with Crista, it took me quite a while to get used to the very different way of using my hands. Instead of holding a phone or using a computer or calculator, I was holding an infant and a bottle. It's a major change. Not interacting with other adults during the day was also really hard to adjust to."

It may take a while for that feeling of withdrawal and deprivation to congeal. To begin with, there is this beautiful miracle beaming up at you, and you may not be thinking one whit about computers and conference calls. But over time, when there is no one else around other than the baby for days on end to "converse" with, you gradually start to feel that something is missing. You begin to have uneasy feelings that you are no longer a productive human being.

There are women who are consummate mothers, and who are consummately happy being mothers 100 percent of the time. They love it, they are experts at it, they get fulfilled by it. Leona O'Hare is one.

For the mother who has worked out of choice and enjoyed it, however, eventually she will come up against a set of feelings about not having that world around her.

Before the birth of the baby, your roles, duties and responsibilities as a two-member team were clearly established and familiar. After the birth of the baby, the name of the game has changed and the same ground rules no longer apply. And if you assume they do, you'll usually run into conflict. You can still go to the movies or the beach, but if you're going to take the baby, you also have to take the diapers, the diaper disposal, the lotion, the cornstarch, the change of clothes for baby and yourself, the toys, and maybe even the playpen. By the time you pack the car, there is no room for the baby or you, *and* it's time to turn around and go home—in your own driveway!

On a more serious note, one mother talked to me about her anger at the fact that nothing had changed for her husband.

"Right before the baby was born, Larry gave me a lecture on how he was never going to miss a morning of racquetball at the health club. And he hasn't! Before the baby was born, he used to leave the house at 5:30 in the morning to meet his friends for exercise and come home at 7:00 in the evening. Now, a year and a half after our first child, he is still leaving the house every morning at 5:30 and getting home at 7:00 or 7:30 at night.

"For the past 11 years of my life I worked full-time. Now suddenly I'm home alone with an infant all day long while my friends are still working. I have no one to talk to. By the time Larry gets home, some 14 hours after leaving in the morning, I'm in tears and exhausted. His response is, 'What did you do all day?' He asks me that practically every day!"

Larry is trying to keep the exact same game rules in their relationship that applied before the birth of their first child, leaving his wife to make the major adjustments. Even more harmful is his attitude: by denying the legitimacy of Elaine's "workday" with the baby, he is leaving her in an emotional vacuum. When I talked to him about his attitude, he explained that he recognized how hard she had worked in her career (she was a graphic artist in an ad agency), but he just couldn't see how "staying at home with a baby could possibly be challenging—let alone tiring!"

Well, needless to say, it was easy to cook up a solution to this misperception. With Larry's very grudging agreement, Elaine packed her bags and left for Santa Barbara for two days—leaving Larry home to take care of the baby. By the time Elaine returned, Larry was a total wreck. He hadn't slept more than one hour at a time for two nights. The baby's crying, he willingly admitted, had set his teeth on edge and left him wild-eyed and short-fused. The lack of adult interaction made him feel "disoriented," and he began to give thanks that his part of this set-up was so much easier than Elaine's. Larry had finally recognized that the game plan had changed, and that if his relationship with his wife were to survive, he had better learn some new rules.

To Know Them Is to Love Them?

Because you've given birth to a baby does not mean you cannot have the same fluctuating feelings about the baby that you have about other things. The expectation of instantly loving the newborn is one of the most damaging expectations of new parenthood. Parents will condemn themselves for not feeling a rush of loving feelings, occasionally even lapsing into severe depressions because they could not get their loving mechanisms to operate on demand. It may take months or even years to be, feel, or love like a parent. Maybe it will happen with the first fever, fall, or smile. Perhaps it is felt only when the child is sleeping; or possibly not until you wave goodbye on the first day of preschool.

I've sat across from many parents and said to them, "You know, there are going to be days when you're not going to like your baby." Parents are always relieved to hear that said straight out. "Some days, you're not going to feel like *liking*, and it's okay because there are going to be days when the baby doesn't like you either."

I remember one mother, in particular. She had come for a consultation looking frustrated and on-edge. It had been one of those weeks—I could see it in her face before she spoke a word. Even before I asked her the reason for her visit, I simply told her that she wasn't always going to like being a mother, and she wasn't always going to like taking care of her baby. She cried with relief. It was her strongest feeling at that moment in time, yet it had seemed so unutterable.

Once relaxed, she told me about the benefit she had attended in a posh Beverly Hills restaurant. She hadn't been able to get a babysitter, primarily because she hadn't really tried. She still believed she was the only really competent caretaker for her baby. Before even leaving the house, her five-month-old had spit up on her cobalt blue silk blouse. Then, in the middle of the afternoon gala, the pampers had sprung a leak and out gushed baby poop all over her skirt. But she had learned to come prepared! She had a spare change of clothes in the car.

Now, after acknowledging the worst—that sometimes she didn't like being a mother and all the endless tasks that came with it—she could laugh about the incident and take it in stride. *Resiliency* has got to be the primary staying quality of parenting!

What about the new mother who has never experienced a baby's spitting up? Now, because her baby spits up frequently, she walks around a great deal of the time with the smell of vomit on her clothes. It doesn't make her a bad parent if she dislikes the spit-up and says so. It just makes her a normal, sensate human being.

One mother's story reflects a more serious experience of not feeling love instantly, on demand. It also shows how the expectation of feeling love only compounds a volatile situation by adding insult (judgment) to injury.

"I had to have a Cesarean. My son came out crying, and proceeded to cry for the next six months! When the nurse first brought him to me she said in her sweet, gooey tone, 'I'd like you to meet your son.' But he was screaming, shrieking, and I thought, 'Oh, God help me!' His screams gave me goose bumps—I felt so powerless.

"This is going to sound really strange. I just remembered the other day that for the first three weeks of my son's life, I called him 'Mister.' When he was brought to me in the hospital I would say, 'Hi, Mister, how are you?'

"Christopher—his real name—had to stay in the hospital for two weeks after his birth. I had to leave the hospital without my baby. When I got home, I felt like I had nothing. Postpartum depression set in, but I still felt excited at the prospect of finally bringing my baby home. But when I did, all he did was scream and scream and scream. I couldn't get him to stop screaming. I rocked him, I walked him, I soothed him, I played soft music for him. *Nothing* seemed to help.

"This went on for months—I couldn't leave the house, I couldn't go anywhere with Christopher. The worst was at night. We lived in an apartment building and his cries sounded like they were coming through a megaphone. People would complain. My husband needed his sleep for work the next day, so the entire burden of coping with the crying fell to me. After a few months of this pattern, I began to feel like I was losing it.

"What made things even worse was that Christopher would stop crying for other people. In desperation to get out of the house, I would take him to my sister's. She'd insist on watching him for an hour or so while I went shopping or to the gym. When I'd get back she would calmly report, 'He was fine, no problem.' That made me feel *really* inadequate.

"Other first-time mothers I knew weren't having nearly the problems I was having. It had to be my fault. It had to be that I didn't love him enough. The truth is, I couldn't even relate to the word *love*—I was just trying to survive day-by-day."

This mother was no monster. She wanted to have a baby and she prepared for the birth. But nothing could prepare her for several months of crying. (Chapter 5 discusses various ways of dealing with crying.) Now, at the age of two, Christopher is finally settling down and she is beginning to enjoy being with him. The two of them took an airplane trip back east last month—something she would never have dreamed possible six months ago.

"Christopher has become a real self-entertainer," she reported. "He looked at books, he looked at people, he played peek-a-boo, he was enthralled by the plane— and he *didn't* cry. I am so grateful to be past that stage—or whatever it was—it felt more like an eternity. I feel like I'm just beginning to get to know my son."

What were the causes of Christopher's problems? Probably a number of complex factors, both physical and emotional in nature. One thing was for certain. The mother's severe feelings of guilt and inadequacy about her lack of loving feelings didn't help the situation one bit. I had several conferences with her during the roughest times, and each time I emphasized that it was perfectly natural for her to feel frustrated and even unloving. No human being can listen to a screaming infant day in and day out and still harbor an abundance of tender, loving sentiments. You just have to take it on the faith that you do love your child—even if you don't feel the warm flush of it!

I am reporting the really difficult times my mothers have had with their babies because I believe those are the experiences that need the most support and acceptance. You all know how to be happy about your baby. You all know how to cope with the easier times. Being confronted with the grueling reality of a constantly crying baby takes incredible guts and stamina; it also takes a great deal of emotional and psychological strength to handle the very *un*loving feelings you might have in the process.

Another mother described her struggle to survive four months of crying and find the light at the end of her tunnel:

"I was 30 when I had my first baby. I had a very long, hard labor and gave birth naturally. After the birth I was in so much pain that I didn't even want to see my baby for 24 hours. I kept thinking, *I can't believe women go through this*! I was scared to leave the hospital and, for the first time in my life, I had no idea how I was going to cope. Basically, I was in shock. When I tried to dress the baby to leave the hospital, I began hyperventilating and had to lay down.

"Hunter was born the week before Christmas. We had a span of about ten days when things went smoothly. My eyes were drooping from the night feedings, but I expected that. Then he developed colic and began crying all day long—and I mean that, literally. If he was awake, he was crying. He never just lay contentedly in his crib and looked around at his surroundings.

"At first I comforted myself with the thought, *This is just temporary*. But as the days turned into weeks, I began to feel pretty desperate. Almost every day I would lock myself in the bathroom, sobbing, feeling like I was going to lose control and harm the baby. I got hot flashes and anxiety attacks. I would put Hunter down in the crib and feel like screaming at him, "Just stop it!", but he would just keep crying. Then, after he would finally fall asleep, I would look at his sweet, peaceful face and wonder how I could have felt such rage an hour before.

"I did finally lose control, and our poor dog took the brunt of it. It was about 7 or 8 o'clock in the evening. My husband wasn't home from work yet and Hunter was just finishing one of his long crying spells. I picked him up to take him downstairs and rounded the corner, heading down the staircase. The dog got in the way. . .I tripped and grabbed onto the railing to keep from falling. . .Hunter started crying. . .the cat let out a wail…and I let loose and kicked the dog—hard, very hard. It was horrible. I felt like a witch.

"Through most of Hunter's first four months, I felt lost, like there was no one I could talk to. My husband did his best to make me feel supported, and he certainly pitched in whenever he could. But he was at work for 10 hours a day, and I was home alone with Hunter for 10 hours a day. My calls to you [Dr. Buddy] helped, but the moment I hung up the phone to try something new, I felt isolated again.

"I *wanted* to have a baby, and I *wanted* to be a full-time mother. I had officially resigned from my career to have Hunter and I saw myself being a full-time mother for at least the first three years. It never occurred to me that I would end up struggling with *not liking* my own baby so much of the time. It devastated me not to feel the kind of motherly love I thought I ought to be feeling."

Three-and-a-half months into this mother's night-mare, I suggested that she go back to work (they had the financial ability to allow her this option). I knew that her career had been a major part of her life, and I knew that she desperately needed to feel good about herself again in some context. It would be better for her *and* for Hunter. At first she resisted, saying that being a mother was her job now. Then, after sitting with the idea for a week or so, she called me one day sounding like a different person.

"I've been facing the fact that this just isn't working. I looked at myself, I looked at my beautiful baby, and husband, and house and realized, *Hey, I'm not happy— I'm miserable.* I phoned my boss and we made arrangements for me to work three days a week. I don't even feel guilty any more. I've suffered so much and tried so hard—I just have to do what feels right to me— and going back to work feels very, very right."

She scoured her city for the right caretaking help and resumed her career. Hunter continued to cry into his fourth month, and then slowly began tapering off. It seemed the more mobile he got, the less he cried. Now, at nine months of age, Hunter rarely cries. His mother thoroughly enjoys being with him and getting to know him. Most of all, she enjoys the effortless flush of loving feelings she gets now. She summarizes:

"I had an incredibly tough time those first months with Hunter, but I'm no longer embarrassed to admit it or talk about it. Somehow or other, I made it through. I'm just beginning to feel really comfortable as a mother. I've made the adjustments; I've gotten help and gone back to work. I feel like myself again. We are even thinking about having a second baby. I've learned so much from Hunter, and this time, I *know* what I am getting into!"

Love for your baby is not a bionic ray that strikes you in the hospital, infusing you with immediate, everlasting rapture. Love is the product of many things that happen in a progression of days and nights with your child. We have idealized love through the auspices of movies, the media, and mothers-in-law for so long that our ideals must surely crumble in the face of a far starker reality. Loving your child is nothing more and nothing less than taking all the indicated *actions* in caring for him or her.

Somehow, we have managed to separate the *feeling of love* from *the taking of action*. We idealize love but we take actions for granted. I am suggesting that they are one and the same thing.

Worrying about whether you are loving your child enough is meaningless. Your love *unfolds*, just as each day does, ever providing you with the opportunity to demonstrate it—scream by scream, tear by tear, and joy by joy.

Now take a few minutes to consolidate your perspective. See where you are at in terms of assumptions, expectations and values. Answer honestly, marking your first impulse with a check. It is best *not* to deliberate over each statement. Give "right-brain" answers rather than "left-brain" ones!

Checking Your Myths At The Door

		Often	Sometimes	Rarely	Never
1)	I feel like I never do enough.	❑	❑	❑	❑
2)	I wonder why parenting seems so hard for me.	❑	❑	❑	❑
3)	I feel guilty that I don't have time to do more special activities with my child.	❑	❑	❑	❑

	Often	Sometimes	Rarely	Never
4) I feel selfish when I want to do something just for myself.	❑	❑	❑	❑
5) I feel guilty whenever I leave my child with a sitter.	❑	❑	❑	❑
6) I feel like I have to carefully supervise my child's eating habits.	❑	❑	❑	❑
7) I feel like I have to carefully supervise my child's dressing habits.	❑	❑	❑	❑
8) I worry that I'm not giving my child enough opportunities to bring out all of his/her potential.	❑	❑	❑	❑
9) I wish my child had a different temperament.	❑	❑	❑	❑
10) I wish my child had different likes and dislikes.	❑	❑	❑	❑
11) I encourage my child to excel in everything he/she attempts.	❑	❑	❑	❑
12) I encourage my child to compete to his/her utmost in everything he/she attempts.	❑	❑	❑	❑
13) I catch myself comparing my child to other children.	❑	❑	❑	❑
14) I try to read everything available on childrearing.	❑	❑	❑	❑
15) When a crisis erupts, my first inclination is to see what the books say.	❑	❑	❑	❑

	Often	Sometimes	Rarely	Never

16) I feel that my hunches cannot really be trusted. ❏ ❏ ❏ ❏

17) I feel that my pediatrician knows more than I do about my child's behavior. ❏ ❏ ❏ ❏

18) I turn to my family and friends for advice. ❏ ❏ ❏ ❏

19) I feel that common sense is not enough in handling the problems my child presents to me. ❏ ❏ ❏ ❏

20) I am angry that things aren't like they used to be. ❏ ❏ ❏ ❏

21) If I just tried harder, I could make things be the way they used to be. ❏ ❏ ❏ ❏

22) I feel like less a person now than when I was working. ❏ ❏ ❏ ❏

23) I wish our sex life had more life to it. ❏ ❏ ❏ ❏

24) At the end of the day I ask myself, "What did you do all day?" ❏ ❏ ❏ ❏

25) My partner doesn't understand why I'm so tired all the time. ❏ ❏ ❏ ❏

26) My partner sticks to his (her) "pre-baby" schedule. ❏ ❏ ❏ ❏

27) It upsets me that I don't feel how I expected to feel about our baby. ❏ ❏ ❏ ❏

	Often	Sometimes	Rarely	Never
28) I believe that parents should have warm, loving feelings about their baby, no matter what.	❏	❏	❏	❏
29) I wish I tolerated my baby's crying better.	❏	❏	❏	❏
30) I should be able to make my baby stop crying by figuring out what she (he) needs.	❏	❏	❏	❏
31) When I can't make my baby stop crying, I get very agitated.	❏	❏	❏	❏
32) When I can't make my baby stop crying, I feel like a failure.	❏	❏	❏	❏
33) I should like being a mother all of the time.	❏	❏	❏	❏
34) I want to go back to work at least part-time—but I don't think I should.	❏	❏	❏	❏
35) I feel guilty about how I feel about my baby.	❏	❏	❏	❏

Whew. Now sit back and evaluate your responses. For starters, if most of your checks fall in the "Rarely" or "Never" columns, you're either in excellent shape myth-wise, or you're answering from an idealistic rather than realistic position. Let's hope it means that you've got a thoroughly realistic view of what parenting is all about.

If you've got a substantial number of checks in the "Often" and "Sometimes" columns, you may need to do some major housecleaning. First, see where your checks cluster. Statements 1-13 concern the Perfect Parent Myth, statements 14-19 reflect the Expert Myth, statements 20-26 represent the area of Relationship Myths, and 27-36 reflect the Instant Love Myth. You may find that you are well-grounded about your relationship but pretty enmeshed in assumptions and expectations of perfect parenting. Or, you may find that the expert myth is your weakest area, with instant love pulling up a close second. Take each area in which your responses cluster in the first two columns and begin to flush them out. Talk with your partner, write by yourself, talk with a friend—but begin to get clear on the assumptions, values and expectations that comprise these core myths. You will find that the more *aware* you become of the myths underlying your parenting, the less you will actually live them.

Now, let's roll up our sleeves and tackle the bane of every parent's day—DISCIPLINE.

4 ❧

Winning At Discipline

Limits are organic. You reset them, just as you prune and cultivate a rose bush, redirecting them to fit the ever-changing situation of a living, growing being. Absolute rules are a shorthand that will net you nothing but absolute problems in the long run.

How many of you wait for a crisis to discipline? Then, under conditions of dire chaos, you lay down unreasonable, unbreachable rules—only to bristle and rage at the dissention and rebellion that follow. You end up feeling completely ineffective and confused, ruled by the child you are supposed to be raising.

Or, perhaps your style of disciplining is to *continually* oversee your child's actions. Rather than waiting for a particular blow-up, you feel it is necessary to intervene often—*very* often—in order to give your child plenty of parameters. You may even go so far as to "hover" over your child, as if each and every action were your responsibility to mold to perfection. You end up feeling as if you have no life of your own—and you don't! Almost all of your time and energy goes into the activity of parenting your child in accordance with a very impossible, very invisible, inner standard.

Today, this moment, your communication with your children may be dreadful. The lines of communication have become like abused arteries, clogged for years with emotional stoppage. Just as a sufferer of arteriosclerosis (hardening of the arteries) must gradually decrease his consumption of dietary villains in order to open his metabolic channels, so must the parent gradually replace bribery, indulgence, and over-parenting with fair, firm, and *consistent* discipline. You can start anywhere, any time. It's not easy, but neither is being constantly manipulated by your kids (the consumed parent); neither is living in the surveillance mode every hour of every day (the consuming parent).

No matter what topic I am asked to speak about at parent meetings—from sleeping problems, to eating problems, to school problems, to issues of over-parenting—the "problem" of *discipline* is always raised. Invariably, the assigned topic fades away as parents veer toward the area of greatest urgency.

"How do I enforce discipline?"

"When do I enforce it?"

"Do I hit?"

"Do I scream?"

"Do I talk?"

"Do I ignore?

"How do I make my child understand that *I* am the parent?"

"How do I get back my control?"

"How can I stop being so obsessed with my child's behavior?"

I begin by telling parents about the consumed/ consuming cycle of parenting and how it can affect their attempts at disciplining.   At the source of our different styles of parenting is some kind of *root assumption* about the nature of parenting. Before you can make any substantial changes in how you discipline and how you parent, you must uncover your root assumption about parenting.

Do you have the idea that good parenting means being focused entirely on your child's needs, and that your own needs are not important or are selfish (*consumed*)?

Do you believe that good parenting means constant vigilance, surveillance, direction, protection and control of the child (*consuming*)?

As I have said, the first step in finding answers to the discipline dilemma is to identify whether you are in the consumed or consuming portion of the cycle. Either results in a loss of control.

The consumed parent needs to ask the question:
"How did I lose control in the first place?"
The consuming parent needs to ask a different question:
"How did I get so over-involved and over-controlling?"

Let's take a look at how each style of parenting affects the disciplining of your children.

The Consumed Parent

Consumed parents fear discipline. They fear that if they exercise control, they will lose their child's love. The consumed parent most often feels out of control— and *is* out of control. Control has shifted to the manipulative child who, through an infinite variety of behaviors, has found a way to get almost anything he wants. The parent is left feeling *very* unparentlike — even un-*person*like, for she has lost some of her rights as an individual. She tends to ruminate over each and every intervention. Did I act too quickly? Should I be less emotional? Did I injure my child's self-esteem? Always on the defensive, she avoids establishing any rules for fear that the rules will forever squash her child's developing individuality.

The Consumed Disciplinarian

As a parent, do you find yourself answering yes to many of the following questions?

- Are you afraid that discipline will cause you to lose the love of your child?
- Are you hesitant to enforce limits in public places as well as at home?
- Do you feel like you're treading water every time you attempt to discipline?
- Are you afraid that limit-setting will land your child on a therapist's couch 20 years from now?
- Are you afraid that listening to your own needs will make you a selfish parent and deprive your child?
- Is your stomach in a knot whenever you attempt to bring order into the household?
- Do you doubt many of the actions you take with your child?

If these questions make you feel uncomfortable or defensive, then you may be a consumed disciplinarian—a contradiction in terms, which you can begin rectifying this very moment.

The Consuming Parent

The consuming parent, by contrast, appears to discipline more easily because she is accustomed to controlling the child's behavior *in the name of love.* Rules and inflexible standards are the guidelines. For her, discipline may take the form of constant instructions as to how to behave, frequent cajoling, endless planned activities and expectations—all of which swirl around the child in an ever-present cloud of direction and control. Of course, this is not true discipline. This is *over-parenting* that, in essence, rob's the child of her own autonomy.

The Consuming Disciplinarian

As a parent, do you find yourself answering yes to many of the following questions?

- Do you enforce absolute rules about different types of behavior regardless of the circumstances? ("My child should always...wear long pants in a shopping mall...be polite and responsive to new people...eat neatly...be happy with new experiences.")
- Are you frequently telling your child what to do, even in areas she is capable of handling? (A five-year-old is quite capable of dressing herself for play, but the consuming parent will find it difficult to let her do so if the child picks an unfit outfit.)
- Do you automatically evaluate many of your child's behaviors as good or bad and then try to change them?
- Do you reprimand your child even for insignificant things? ("Don't play with your toes so much!")

If these questions make you feel uncomfortable or defensive, then you may be a consuming disciplinarian—ineffective due to overkill. You can begin rectifying this pattern this very moment.

For the consuming parent, discipline becomes ineffective because the parent is *always* telling the child how to behave. The consumed parent, by contrast, only intervenes when it is absolutely necessary to control the child's uncontrollable behavior—and then often succumbs to bribery and temper tantrums that result in a final defeat.

AXIOMS to ponder:

> *The consumed parent is always fighting to get control back from the child.*

> *The consuming parent is in control too much of the time.*

The problems our two fictional parents encounter when enforcing discipline are going to be different. The consumed parent needs to learn how to assert herself, how to give up her fear that the child is not going to love her, how to set limits. The consuming parent, by contrast, needs to learn how to "back off" from the child, give more space, discipline in selected areas while giving some experience of "free reign" in others.

Confusing Love and Discipline

I have found that, most often, parents lose control because they *confuse love and discipline*. This confusion can come from the fear that if you exercise control, you'll *lose* your child's love; or that exercising control *proves* your love. Both sides of this confused coin net ineffective discipline.

Because most of us do struggle with confusion over love and discipline, we spend a lot of time feeling anxious and guilty about the discipline we do enforce. It feels haphazard; it feels sporadic; it feels too controlling; it feels too strict or too lenient. We think if we discipline too much, that means we're not showing love; and if we overindulge, we're impeding the child's maturity.

Every direction in which we turn leads us back to guilt. I know, because I struggled with it through three children of my own, and with the nearly 4,000 families I have treated over the years. To make your child go to bed without a meal is anguishing, pure and simple; even sending him to his bedroom produces accusatory pangs. Will he turn to drugs before the age of 12? Is he going to need a psychiatrist when he's 30?

There is no question in my mind that the hardest part about parenting is disciplining. From the first day you take the baby home from the hospital, until the day when your child crosses your threshold to his or her own life, you are hoping that you won't lose control *and* hoping that you won't *misuse* whatever control you manage to create. I thought that raising kids would be one long fantasy:

> *We would feed them, put them to bed, walk with them, play with them, dress them up prettily; they would go to school and get smart; and then they would leave home and we would be through!*

What I found out was that whatever we fed them, they didn't like; they didn't want to go to bed when we wanted them to; they could have cared less about the walk we wanted to take them on; they hated to be dressed at all, let alone prettily; they went to school and got smart, but then they always thought they were smarter than we were; and when they left home, it wasn't really the end—it was just the beginning of a new chapter!

The disciplinary approaches I am going to present in this chapter are the result of 28 years of experience as a father and a pediatrician. The methods are straightforward and easy to describe—but I do not pretend to claim that they are easy to execute. Whenever a parent enforces discipline, he or she is confronted with emotional responses. There is turmoil in applying *any* type of discipline, no matter how "ideal" or "proven."

I am providing one framework as a possible approach to discipline: identifying where you are in the consuming/consumed cycle, understanding how that affects your discipline, and making the desired changes in your attitudes and behavior. But within this framework you will still need to go through a private process of coping with your own emotional responses to it. And ultimately, you will have to answer the most important question, "Is this the right approach *for us?*" Disciplining is an intensely personal activity with intensely serious consequences. As parents, you must find a way that is effective *and* comfortable for you.

Before you can even hope to be successful disciplinarians, you have got to realize that *it's okay for your kids to not like you once in a while, just like it's okay for you to not like your children once in a while.* The love is always there; the bond is always there. But none of us *always* likes being around another person. We have our good days and our bad days. So do children and parents. The sooner you can live with that and not feel guilty, the easier the job becomes. Once you give up the notion of having to like and be liked every single day, you will feel a new freedom that comes from being honest and real.

Bribery: The Road Most Traveled

Bribery is the surest sign that you are confusing love and discipline, and it is the best possible way to fail at discipline. Even the Bible says, "an eye for an eye"—in this case, a matinee ticket to *Star Wars* for drying the dishes. Better still, take him to the movies even if he doesn't want to go—you can bargain for other chores over popcorn and Goobers. His promises may not last as long as the candy, but the movie will give you time to think up new strategy—like not playing outside until he loads the dishwasher. (Maybe that should have been "no playing inside"—he's got a stereo, television set and tape deck in his room!)

Or, tell him if he doesn't do his chores, you'll send him to bed without dinner—but, he does that often himself! Perhaps the best thing to do is wait until he wants something so badly, so urgently, that he'll do just about anything to get it. The ice cream man is two blocks away? Okay, but not until he eats five spoons of applesauce and feeds that cat! And if he wants those two friends to sleep over, he'll have to change the hamster cage and walk the dog if they can stay up for the Midnight Special.

As you're finally sitting down reviewing your day, you can't for the life of you remember how two friends sleeping over became a neighborhood slumber party in the den. Oh, yes—he said he'd clean up his room if you said yes. He didn't...because.

A startling example of bribery instead of discipline which is brought to my attention frequently in my professional life is the mother who complains about taking the child to the market. One mother joked about how every time she went to the market, it cost her more money to keep her child quiet than it did to buy the family's groceries. How does the straightforward task of marketing get blown into an out-of-control situation? And all by the doings of a little person weighing 30 pounds or less?

The first time the child goes to the market and screams because she wants something, the mother hands her one piece of gum, and lo, she is quiet. The second time she cries a little louder, and when Mother gives her one piece of gum, she screams for a package. On the third trip to the market, she wants more than just the gum, so she screams and throws a temper tantrum on the floor. She gets the comic book and the coloring book.

The besieged mother gives in because she is embarrassed by her child's behavior in the market. When the fourth marketing trip arrives and mother says, "We're going to the market," guess what her little girl says. She says, "I'll go, but only if I can have...."

And it is here that the parent becomes the slave and the child the master. Now it is the little girl who is dictating the terms of the event; she is saying, in effect, "If you want me to go shopping with you and keep my mouth shut, then you'll have to do such-and-such for me." Even before the age of two—as soon as he is physically able to leap out of a cart—a child can be wielding enough power to keep the shopping mom on the brink of a breakdown with each trip.

Yet kids can be so charming, so unabashedly endearing, that the screams and shrieks they assaulted you with in the morning are forgotten when they need a ride to the skating rink at noon. Later, when you feel like you've been had, you think, "Wait a minute, there have got to be some limits." But where in the vicious cycle of a child's seeming tyranny against us do we set these limits?

We hear a lot about child abuse today, but I think we also need to be aware of *parent abuse*. Parent abuse is the situation that happens when children literally enslave their parents through manipulative behavior. This manipulative behavior is seeded in parental bribes that tell children *they* have ultimate control. It is probably the most common cause of "parent burn-out," and brings most parents to their wits end on the average of once a day.

Just What is Discipline?

Discipline. What is it? Let me begin by telling you what I know it is *not*. It is not watching over your child's every move. It is not responding in the anger of the moment and whacking the kid on the back of the head. It is not throwing shoes at the door instead of at the child because you are ready to burst with frustration. It is not calling your child "stupid," or "dumb," or an "idiot" for not saving his allowance or forgetting to turn off his computer. Even the most loving and patient parents can lose their tempers and fall prey to name-calling now and then, simply by virtue of the fact that parenting can be an unyieldingly hard job.

One time when we were on vacation in Montana, my eight-year-old son intentionally tripped his mother. I was so incensed, I lifted him up by his ears right there on the street corner and shook him. And that was wrong, because I was acting in the moment of my anger.

In my mind, *discipline is something to teach*; it is not a *punishment* to enforce. Childhood, in essence, is a training period, and I cannot overemphasize *who* is the teacher and *who* is the student. With children of all ages, this relationship all too easily gets reversed so that *you* wind up being the student, not the teacher! The manipulative child can turn you around in a minute; it's easy for you to anticipate this potential pitfall by knowing the child and avoiding the manipulation. *You are the teacher*, and the child is the student, learning.

By discipline, I mean structuring the training that is necessary to guide a child toward effectiveness and enjoyment in daily living. All too often, we equate discipline with punishment, rigidity, or injustice. With such a view, we feed the fear that if we employ it, our children will be stymied in their individuality and end up not loving us. On the other hand, we fear that if we don't employ it, we will lose control over our children and they will lose respect for us at best, and at worst, end up in Juvenile Hall.

But isn't it the undisciplined individual who is truly stymied? Isn't it the adult who cannot effectively navigate a single day of living (and there are many) who is distressfully handicapped? Without discipline, the adult has only a false freedom, if any, and is usually aware of a lack of guidance and control over himself and the events of his life. An undisciplined adult is unsure of himself, and uncertain of what to do, what not to do, and how to live.

Discipline is a way of *impressing* our children, not molding them. As psychologist Richard Farson says:

> We have treated our children as if we could shape them the way a sculptor shapes clay; but that's not the way it is. It's more like we are running along as we fall on a pile of clay. We leave an impression which is distinctly us, but we have very little control over what it looks like.

Imagine, if you will, a sand castle. We really have no control over the elements that can buffet this sand castle, yet we pack it and shape it and adjust it, trying to safeguard it against the unknown. If it is disturbed, we reshape and build it up again. A child is somewhat like that sand castle. An overly permissive attitude masquerading as freedom and creativity for the child would allow the sand castle, as it were, to be washed out to sea. Discipline is the ability to persevere in the face of adversity. A child, like a sand castle, needs constant bolstering, confining, shifting, reinforcement, and reshaping—lest the developmental stages of childhood, like powerful ocean waves, scatter the structure into fragments. The challenges of the elements, just like the challenges of childhood, are different along the way. One day you are confining, another you are reinforcing, and in still another, you are reshaping.

Yesterday's notion of discipline was black-and-white; there were yeses and no's, and you always knew what to expect if you disobeyed a no. Yesterday's parents wanted compliance without questioning—in effect, undaunted obedience. Adults believed (unfortunately, some still do) that children should not disagree, question, or even try to reason until they were young adults themselves.

Today's parents who have uncomfortable memories of this authoritarian style of discipline struggle with added confusion and conflict when trying to shift to less dogmatic approaches. Today's discipline involves the flexible extension of limits in the face of ever-changing challenges. It is not punishment, but rather *the preventive maintenance of living cooperatively* within a family *now* and within a society *tomorrow*.

Rules—the very foundation of yesterday's discipline—were handed down from father-to-father, mother-to-mother. Today, there are more challenges and less rules. Indeed, if there are any effective rules for today's children, they would have to be in the words of William Wordsworth, "very plain and very few indeed." This is because today's parents are not strict disciplinarians. Quite the contrary, you are really worried about your children's feelings. But in your quest to be super parents and to raise super children, you sometimes become oversensitive to behaviors that are the very staple of infancy and childhood.

Our children mustn't cry too long, become upset, feel left out, feel deprived, or have hurt feelings. They mustn't be hungry, thirsty, cold, lonely—they mustn't lose contests, fights, or possessions—*ever*. But the real world into which the young adult steps is not cushioned in such a manner. When we unwittingly raise our children as if it were, we are actually sabotaging the child's possibility of learning to live a full, rich, and *real* life.

Rules have different meanings to the consumed and consuming parent. As I have said, the consumed parent needs to learn how to take a stand and set a limit that cannot be undone by bribery or manipulative behavior. The consuming parent makes use of too many rules and needs to learn how to evaluate which ones are really necessary. The rules need to be flexible and carefully tailored to the unique personality of each child *and* parent. Growing up and parenting are really experiments that go hand-in-hand. Absolute rules create absolute problems later.

Limit-Setting

Rules are different from limit-setting. Limits change with the age, the needs of the child, even with the day's events. Limits are the foundation of childrearing. If the job of raising children is at all do-able—and that is certainly a moot topic—limits are essential in even the attempt.

What are limits? Limits are the expression of our own, genuine convictions. Limits can only be created in relation to the parents' conscientious self-appraisal of what they really believe. What we are doing when we set limits for our children is letting them know where we stand on issues; we are taking a position. *We cannot set limits until we know our own likes, dislikes, and tolerance levels.* Then we can set limits and even change them when necessary.

Consumed and consuming parents face quite different problems in limit-setting. The consumed parent doesn't do it nearly enough, and the consuming parent does it far too much. In a nutshell, my message to the consumed parent is: *Believe in your right to sets limits and learn how to set them.* To the consuming parent I advise: *Loosen up on your limit-setting, "de-rulify" your life, let your child take the lead more often.*

When I begin working with a new parent, I often ask her to make a list of the limits she considers necessary. The list tells me immediately which direction the parent leans toward: consumed or consuming. The consumed parent will cross out as many limits as she adds (you can almost feel the tentativeness rise up off the page), whereas the consuming parent will generate an incredibly lengthy list.

When the parent of a nine-year-old was asked to write down what she viewed as essential for her child, the following list was offered:

1. Must keep room picked up.
2. Must do own laundry.
3. Must unload dishwasher.
4. Must brush teeth after each meal.
5. Must take bath or shower daily.
6. Must feed hamsters, mice, dogs, and cats.
7. Must be home at 6 P.M. for dinner.
8. Must take out garbage.

The parent was then asked to evaluate which items could be tolerably eliminated and which could not (from the parent's standpoint). Could the parent live with the child's messy room? What if the child neglected his laundry? How does the parent really feel about the frequency of bathing? The entire list was re-evaluated. In the end, the parent admitted that a messy room was no problem as long as the child kept his door closed. The laundry, if not done, would be the *child's* dilemma. The dishwasher must be emptied, however, so that other family members would not be inconvenienced. Teeth brushing was essential, but a bath could be skipped once in a while. Children's pets, if not properly cared for, would have to go. A rigid dinner hour, the mother realized, was only reasonable for those who were hungry enough to abide by it. Garbage, however, must be emptied regularly to avoid unsanitary pile-ups.

In the end, cleaning the bedroom, doing laundry, daily bathing and a 6 P.M. dinnertime were taken off the list. Four items remained on the list. These were shared with the child, who also was made aware that neglect brings consequences.

I realize that there are many mothers who are unwilling to tolerate a perpetually messy bedroom. I also realize that many kids don't really know how to keep their things organized and put away. One alternative to the clean versus messy dichotomy is for the mother to help the child reorganize the room together on a periodic basis. That way you're sure your child has the know-how to arrange his or her room, and every so often you are blessed with the view of a neatly organized room.

If, after a while, the child still doesn't pitch in—the garbage is piling up and there's not a clean dish in the house—privileges such as parental taxi service, allowance, television programs and the like, are taken away.

I know that it sounds crazy to ask parents to learn to tolerate conditions they dislike. But part of the process of learning how to successfully discipline for the consuming parent is learning to give more "space" to the child's viewpoint—even when it conflicts when your own. If reducing the number of things you are asking your kids to do establishes a degree of peace that you can live with, then the "pruning" is well worth it. Even more importantly, *when you as parents learn to compromise early, then your children also learn what compromise is, and as they grow older, they are more responsive to your directives and more able to negotiate.*

Adolescence is all about negotiation—from the time your kids put on lipstick and buy their first can of shaving cream, they are in a constant process of attempting to expand their boundaries—which means they are constantly challenging the old boundaries set by you. When you engage your young children in this process of give-and-take—"This is what I would like, but I can give this up if you can agree to this"—then by the time they reach the difficult period of adolescence, they have already learned that negotiating works. So, instead of constant head-on clashes, you get frequent trips to the bargaining table—which is undeniably preferable.

Limits can be enacted the moment the infant begins to test his environment. In the chapter on sleeping, we will see the nine-month-old learning how far he *can't get* with crying. In most cases of limit-setting, the hardest part for parents is the child's response. The child who is sensitive to correction and who answers negatively or whines, "You hurt my feelings," may be trying to dilute the impact of your approach with manipulation. If the child can say, "You've hurt my feelings," shouldn't the parent be able to respond, "What about my feelings?" In this way, the child begins to learn that everyone has feelings, and that *his* feelings alone cannot always determine the course of events.

When you allow manipulative responses to influence the management of a situation, the most virulent kind of parental impotence ensues. Your weapon becomes the child's weapon against you. You've been disarmed.

The greatest peril in this type of disarmament is the "scrambled intuition" you experience as a result. Your reliable intuition about the rightness or wrongness of the situation has become muddled by the child's manipulative behavior, and your set of misguided attitudes and unconscious beliefs about yourself has been triggered. For example, let's take a hard look at just why you are unable to listen to a crying baby.

Your genuine intuitions and convictions originate in the intuitive region of your thinking—the part that knows the baby has been fed, changed, and is safe and sound. Your over-reactions, on the other hand, are generated by that region within that feels inadequate, fearful, and self-doubting. *Mostly we fear not being model parents*, so if we can quiet the baby, we will at least appear to be model parents. Thus we nurture manipulative behavior from the beginning with unnecessary food and cuddling and acquiescence. Setting limits demonstrates our ability to evaluate and reject the negative effects of doting acquiescence in favor of the long-term bonus of our child's maturity.

Setting limits clearly requires the courage of our convictions, the persistence to follow through, and the perseverance to be consistent. It also requires moderation. The consumed parent needs to be aware of the "yes trap"—giving in to demands, whines, and tantrums— while the consuming parent needs to get out of the "no trap"—saying no to almost everything about the child's behavior that doesn't meet the parent's standards of correctness. I can recall the parents who came to my office complaining because their three-year-old was so negative. "I tell her no and she doesn't listen—I ask and she says no." I asked these parents to keep a written record over the next week of how many times they said NO to their little girl. They may have set a record—287 no's per day! As the week progressed, the mother noted a fascinating phenomenon: by the fifth day, when the number of NO's had decreased to 210 per day, the child's negative behavior had also decreased.

How many of us think to say *yes* whenever we spot our toddlers and young children doing things of which we approve? *No* comes out of our mouths automatically—even reflexively. We have to make an effort to give *yeses* equal time! A small investment of agreeableness on our part such as, "*Yes*, how wonderful your dolly is," or "*Yes*, you are playing so well that you may play an extra 15 minutes," or "*Yes*, you may have a friend sleep over" can result in seemingly miraculous changes in behavior.

Let me add quickly, however, that saying yes instead of no is no simple matter in a world where MTV dominates the minds and hearts of our children. MTV quite literally makes your job of parenting a hundred times harder. Saying no to your eight-year-old who *must* have a leather skirt "like Madonna's" pits you against a far greater force than your 60-pound daughter. You find yourself butting heads with a media phenomenon whose influence is both powerful and pervasive. Limit-setting with your child has now become a battle in which Madonna, Michael Jackson and Mick Jagger all play key roles. All the more reason for parents to consciously examine their methods of discipline. The more your limits reflect your deep-held convictions, and are enforced in the context of the principles of flexibility and consistency (discussed later in this chapter)—the greater your chances of positively affecting your child.

Testing Limits

Don't get smug, however, if suddenly and for no apparent reason, your kids can't do enough. They're washing windows, dusting furniture, scouring sinks, and polishing silver. Equate this with those days when you're on fire with energy yourself. But be aware of the test to come. They'll soon be testing to see if your limits are really ironclad, or if you are just as wishy-washy as you used to be.

"Oh, Mom (or Dad), do I have to rake the leaves

today after I vacuumed, polished, washed and dusted yesterday?", the child asks, feeling that justice is surely on his side.

The answer is *yes!* If you back off, you're allowing manipulative behavior to become a habit again. Believe it or not, a sporadically industrious child does so partly to use his industriousness as a wedge against the everyday routines he doesn't want to do. Kids are pros at convincing us that if we don't let them off the hook, we don't love or appreciate them. The only way to depotentiate our own hook-in to such common accusations is by knowing they are just another form of manipulation.

The child asking for gum, toys, or coloring books in the market is *testing*—and the parent who is giving her the goods is *failing* the test. What should you as a parent do? Chances are, give that first piece of gum, get the shopping over with, and get home! The next time you go shopping, give the child one more chance to behave, *but no gum—because with the second piece of gum you give, you're trapped.* And the third time you go shopping, your child doesn't go. You make arrangements for someone to babysit for that hour, or you go shopping at night and your spouse stays home with the child. Whatever. *But you don't take the child again, because all you're teaching him or her is how to be manipulative. It's normal for kids to test. Testing is one thing. But when the testing is successful for the child, that's when manipulative behavior comes into effect.* In other words, the child tests to get the gum, and if she's gratified, her behavior then becomes manipulative. Or, to put it yet another way, the child learns manipulative behavior every time the parent fails the "testing test."

The consuming parent might encounter a different version of this problem and also wind up failing the "testing test." Often, the consuming parent confuses testing behavior that should be quelled with testing behavior that is part of the child's normal exploration of the environment. The parent will view both types of behavior as the same and attempt to discipline both. This cuts the child off from a wide range of healthy, assertive, creative energy and also dissipates the effect of discipline when it is advisable. So many no's and so much control begin to have less and less impact while generating more and more resistance.

I think it is extremely important to emphasize that *testing is natural behavior for the child*. The child is not trying to besiege the parent, although when a child versed in manipulative behavior is testing you to the limit, you begin to feel like you're being tortured! The one saving grace in the testing situation is the fact that you as the parent really do have ultimate control over the testing tug-of-war. I think a lot of parents get caught up in frenzied emotional responses to the behavior because they forget that the child is really just proceeding along a normal growth principle of exploring the boundaries of his or her control. Instead, they can learn to say NO in a voice that is firm but free of condemnation.

We all test, even as adults. My mother used to test me, even at the age of 75. She was forever calling me and saying, "The reason you don't come over is because you don't love me." Even when I visited her twice a week, she would say the same thing. When I used to call her after not having talked to her for two weeks because I was a resident and on call most of the time she'd say, "What's wrong? How come I haven't heard from you?"

I'd say, "Well, Mom, it's really hard talking on a hospital phone while I'm making rounds!"

Then my mother would yell to my dad, "Phil, did you know Bud's in the hospital?"

Then she'd say, "You're only calling because you have to."

I'd say, "No. I'm calling to find out how you are. But if you think I have to, I'll hang up." I was testing her.

She'd say, "Go ahead." So I'd hang up, and she'd call me back. My mother and I had similar personalities—we usually hung up on each other about the same time!

Testing is by far the earliest discipline problem that parents encounter; and it is probably the most chronic and consistent one as well. Every now and then, though, an experience will "kick in" and the child will make a quantum leap, behaviorally. In restaurants, my adolescent son had the habit of scanning the menu and always picking the most expensive sandwich. One day we were eating out, and I was tired of it because he never finished eating the sandwich. I said, "I want you to have anything you want, but the deal is, you have to finish eating it. All of it. Okay?"

He said, "Sure, Dad," and selected a giant club sandwich—the most expensive sandwich on the menu. I knew that, even though he was a good eater, he wouldn't be able to finish it. He took about four bites of it and said he didn't like the bacon.

I said, "Did you read what was in it?"

He said, "Yeah."

"Then why did you order it?" I asked. I knew why. He wanted to see how far his power went. I made him eat the bacon and I proved my point. He was through testing me, on this point at least, because he understood from then on what I was trying to tell him. He could eat anything he *truly* wanted. It had nothing to do with how expensive it was, but it did have to do with my power to refuse to participate in his manipulative behavior. But that's testing, and it's perfectly normal behavior. He wasn't plotting to infuriate me at each restaurant trip; he was simply seeing how far his childhood boundaries extended in this particular area.

Distinguishing Between Types of Manipulative Behavior

Manipulative behavior is a staple of childhood. It is probably the most consistently frequent behavior parents encounter. Consumed and consuming parents alike will be challenged to the core by the normal manipulations of a growing child who is checking out and testing his environment. What differs is the typical mode of response for our two groups of parents: Both tend to allow the manipulation. The difference is, the consuming parent counters with additional manipulation, while the consumed parent falls further into the defensive zone. Both parents need to break their patterns of response. A simple way to begin is by distinguishing between the different types of manipulative behaviors rather than responding in the same manner across the board.

Naturally there are going to be times when the child's manipulative behavior is really an expression of a problem that needs to be dealt with on an emotional and/or physical level. As parents, you need to distinguish when the behavior is suggesting an emotional problem of some kind, or when the behavior is indicative of a possible physical, organic problem. Because children don't know how to express their feelings directly, they will often use manipulative behavior as a tool of communicating a message that they want their parents to hear. For example, the child who isn't hungry at dinnertime for a week straight could be communicating a deeper message about a problem at school or in the family that is causing him to feel badly about himself—or he simply may have discovered the new 7-11 on his bike-ride home from school and is gleefully devouring candy bars and soda pops an hour before dinner. Still another possibility is the presence of some kind of organic problem.

How can parents distinguish between normal, feisty childhood manipulations and those that constitute a cry for help? By using common sense and being willing to observe and examine. Every parent has a "checklist" in her head she automatically scans when the child's behavior changes noticeably. What other events coincide with the loss of hunger at dinnertime? How is the child's appetite for breakfast and lunch? How is his schoolwork? His overall mood and activity level? If his appetite for other meals is fine, and his schoolwork is unchanged, that means the problem isn't pervasive in nature. The parent continues her sleuthing. The change in behavior began when school began.... Now he's riding his bike to school for the first time....He usually rides with his buddy....Sooner or later the smart mother discovers that the child is stopping at 7-11 and putting away a heavy snack—which is exactly what I did at that age!

What if the problem is physical and/or emotional in nature? Children will often express their feelings somatically; tummy aches and headaches can be the child's way of saying he or she is upset or scared by something at home or in school. Or, the physical symptoms may be indicative of an illness of some kind. If the child's complaint persists, it is always safest to check with your physician.

When are parents qualified to help their children deal with emotional problems? Most of the time, parents are the *most* qualified. Parents as a group have received a great deal of bad press recently. With the uncovering of child abuse scandals, we have been confronted with the reality that there are many unfit parents out there—parents who themselves are in desperate need of help and treatment. I do not deny any of this. But I do think that the large group of very fit parents are undermined by the assumption that "experts" are needed at every turn. The parent who has become a parent by choice and who has cared for the child since birth has a wealth of information about the child that constitutes the richest possible source of help. I have found that most of the parents I have worked with over the years (I calculated the time to come to 90,000 parent-hours) possessed ample skills and abilities to deal successfully with the array of emotional problems that arise in their children's lives. I also found that most parents benefitted enormously by simply being told by me—an "expert"— that I thought they knew what they were doing.

It is worthy to note that in a one-hour consultation in which mother and father both participate, the problem would often be resolved without any contributions from me. Simply by taking the time to air their two viewpoints, parents will often discover revelations that lead to solutions they didn't think existed. I believe that providing this kind of atmosphere for parents is one of the most important functions a pediatrician can offer; parents need to feel that their pediatrician is available for this kind of consultation and dialogue. I'm certainly not the only pediatrician in the world to feel this way. The American Academy of Pediatrics is now openly and frequently endorsing this approach of spending quality time with parents.

Flexibility Is the Rule, Consistency Is the Tool

Before you can expect your children to follow a set of rules, you have to have some set of rules for yourselves. Paradoxically, I think one of these rules is, you have to be *flexible*. You have to have one set of rules for one stage of your children's lives and another set of rules for another stage. The consumed parent tends to have too few rules for any of the stages, and the consuming parent tends to rigidly apply rules from one stage over too long a period of time. Both groups of parents need to learn a new kind of discernment.

Let's say you have a house rule that 8:30 P.M. is bedtime, and your child begins to complain. This may be manipulative behavior, or it may be a clue to re-examine a limit. Nobody is right or wrong; it's simply that the child's individual requirements are changing as he develops. Your limit may have become outdated. Revising limits does not undermine consistency. Remember, *limits are like shoes—you can't expect one pair to go from childhood to adolescence. They must be changed regularly for growth and comfort—and at the same time, they must be firmly enforced.*

It's okay for a parent to be wrong. It's great to say, "You know, I think I punished you too hard." We're just as liable as children to overstate something. Kids are always overstating things—that's where the "little white lies" come from. And I think it's okay for parents to do that also, as long as they can come back and say, "I have overdone this."

Many power struggles between parents and children begin with the parent's need to be right. As difficult as it may be to accept authority (particularly if you were raised in an authoritarian household)—even our authority as parents has a right to be questioned. Before we even attempt to set limits, we first must be willing to *relinquish* having our own way.

On his 16th birthday, my son received his older brother's car as a birthday present. The car was no hot rod, but it drove well enough. I was driving home from work that day, up our street which ends in a cul-de-sac. A car whizzed past me in the opposite direction, and I suddenly realized it was my son! I couldn't believe he would drive that fast the first moment he got the keys to the car! He had to be going 45 to 50 m.p.h. on a residential street with lots of playing kids. I was so angry that I turned my car around in a screech and began racing after him down a very steep hill. When I got half-way down the hill, I realized that I was either going to kill him, or we'd both get killed. I stopped chasing him, went back to the house, and waited for him to return.

When he walked in the front door after an hour or so, I grabbed the keys from his hand and said, "You're not getting this car back for a year!" He went to his room all upset. I was furious. I hollered at him that he could have killed and he could have *been* killed. To my way of thinking at that point, he was lucky to be grounded for only a year—it should have been ten years—and his license should have been taken away!

His older brother attempted to intercede at this point. "Dad, how can you take his car away for a whole year?"

"Easy," I said. "He's done something terribly wrong—he could have killed somebody—*ME*, as a matter of fact, because he was driving head-on in my direction. Or you, or your mother, or your sister, or other people. So, to me a year is lucky."

But as I sat and thought about it, I realized that a year wasn't a realistic punishment. The consequence for doing something so terribly wrong had to be effective *now*—not strung out over a year's time, and not so immense that, in all likelihood, he would develop compensatory behaviors—like sneaking our cars, or driving buddy's cars, or whatever. I finally conceded to myself that a year's punishment would only engender a year's worth of resentment and negative behavior. A 16-year-old is simply not going to be without wheels for that length of time.

As I thought about what would constitute effective, constructive discipline, I found out that the big dance was in two weeks. I went into my son's room and said, "I'm not taking your car away for a year, but you're not going to use it for the dance"—which, next to taking away his telephone, was the worst thing I could have done. He got to drive the car to school and then straight home from school. No extra driving around for that period of time. And it worked. In his first driving experience he had learned that he could not get away with hotrodding. The message was, one way or another, you will be caught and disciplined. Part of me remained outraged at his careless driving for several days, and part of me did not like "backing down" from my original position. Yet the objective parent in me was forced to realize—with a little help from my older son—that my punishment would not net any positive consequences. The bottom line was teaching my son to drive safely, and as a parent, I had to put my ego aside in choosing the best way to facilitate that learning.

As parents, we walk a fine line between *discipline* and *authoritarianism*. The one quality that keeps parents safely on the side of fair discipline is flexibility. In the 1960s, kids began to speak out against blind authority— the kind of blind authority that had been the cornerstone of our culture and our parenting. They said, "Wait a minute. Just because you're older doesn't make you smarter. You're my mom and dad, but I've got some feelings, too. I've got some values of my own. Let me express them."

Today's young parents are a product of this shift. They want to be flexible; they don't want to raise their children with the attitude, "If you cross me, I'll smack you." On the other hand, they know that if they are overly permissive, they will lose control. And once they lose control as parents, they're dead ducks. The "Fairytale Nightmare" becomes their reality. In the area of discipline, obviously there are no easy answers. *Limits are organic. You reset them, just as you prune and cultivate a rose bush, redirecting them to fit the ever-changing situation of a living, growing being. Absolute rules are a shorthand that will net you nothing but absolute problems in the long run.*

Now, assuming that you've managed to adjust your "flexibility barometer" to a balanced setting—doing it *less* if you are a *consumed* parent; doing it *more* if you are *consuming*—the next essential "tool-of-the-trade" is *consistency.* Lack of consistency in setting limits accounts for the difficulties encountered in most normal problems: poor eating habits, bedtime battles, toilet training tirades, and so forth. Inconsistency adds to the chaos of the child's world, whereas consistency brings a much needed order to it. As human beings, we are all subject to constant stimuli from our environment, both physical and emotional. Remember that children, too, are subject to the same stimuli, and are not as fully equipped to deal with it as we are. Their inappropriate responses are due very often to their own normal immaturity and the inexperience of their particular age group. Consistency in limit-setting actually helps the child learn to sift and sort through all the input and respond appropriately.

Usually, the consuming parent is very consistent in behavior—in fact, too consistent, as we have noted. For this group of parents, the consistency of control needs to be *loosened* rather than strengthened. Overlook a few misdemeanors, allow your child to dress herself regardless of the outcome, clean up a few spilled food items without getting upset, let her bang around in the kitchen and get flour all over her face in the name of being "Mother's Helper." Don't worry about whether she's doing the task right or wrong. Instead, give her the room to simply explore, experiment, and have a great time.

For the consumed parent, being consistent is easier than you think. Sheer repetition will net you positive results. In the beginning, try not to think too much about what you are enforcing. The rule is, one piece of gum in the market and that is *all*. If your child throws a tantrum for more, out you both go. Proceed blindly on the faith that anything is better than the torture of another public tantrum; anything is better than having to constantly negotiate for your child's cooperation. Be a "consistency robot" for a few days and watch the principle become easier and easier to apply for three very simple reasons:

(1) It works.
(2) It's good for your child.
(3) It's good for you.

Disagreement is Normal

Parents don't always come as a matched set. Often, one parent will tend to be consuming, while the other is busy being consumed. One parent is the disciplinarian; the other parent is easy-going. Then you have a mixture of mixed messages from the parents that leaves the child suspended between two worlds. The mother who says to the child, "You've got to finish your dinner," and the father who counters, "Let him alone!", however, are handing their child a loaded gun of manipulation. This is a very common scene in which the parents then proceed to argue for 15 minutes, during which time the dinner gets utterly cold. Following the big scene, the child usually gets off without finishing his dinner— which is what the problem was all about to begin with. Father or mother becomes terribly angry, taking it as a personal battle and possibly forcing the child to eat something which may have no value. And in the midst of all the bickering, neither parent has thought to ask the child if he or she is even hungry!

If there is disagreement about limit-setting between spouses, take time out—preferably away from the battle front—and discuss the differences of opinion. It is precisely these differences that create mixed messages for the child and undermine the consistency essential in any form of limit-setting on discipline. Talking with each other about the common problems parents face in this always vexing area will help establish the compromise necessary to set up a *united front* against manipulation.

I have a friend who told me that, whenever she and her husband hear about a problem situation concerning someone else's child, they sit down and discuss how they would have handled it. In a way, they are "rehearsing" their responses in the event they encounter a similar situation. Then, if/when such a situation arises, they already know how they want to proceed; they can respond without feeling so overwhelmed by the emotion and trauma surrounding the situation.

For example, my friend's neighbor came over the other day and told her that her 14-year-old, who is good friends with my friend's son, had come home drunk. That evening my friend's husband and she talked about how they would deal with that situation, since it is fairly likely to arise at some point in their future. After their discussion, each knew how the other wanted to respond. It turned out that they had differing views, and so now, before the problem has actually occurred, they can iron out a unified policy for this particular type of problem. This kind of "rehearsal" serves several purposes. For one, parents and children alike become clear on how each one feels about these sensitive situations. For another, a message is communicated to the child that says, in effect, "We are aware that these kinds of things happen, and here is what the consequences will be if they happen in our household." At the same time, however, the discussion serves the third purpose of treating the child like a human being who has legitimate perceptions and responses. The parents are not saying,

"I'll beat your brains out if you do this." Instead, the parents are eliciting the child's viewpoint and engaging him or her in a mature dialogue.

Obviously this approach cannot be fruitfully applied to very young children. Often I hear parents talk to their youngsters as if they were talking to 14-year-olds. Asking a two-year-old, "How do you feel about Daddy leaving?" is expecting a level of verbalization and abstraction that simply isn't available to the child. Giving comfort and affection to the two-year-old while the father is out of town is entirely appropriate; expecting the two-year-old to discuss the situation with you in words is not appropriate.

For some parents, setting limits goes into action in the A.M., for others it's 5 P.M., while still others are at it all day. In any case, be prepared to be challenged, full-throttle, at any time. An example of the five o'clock "challenge":

Mother is preparing dinner. Meanwhile the TV breaks down, Dad calls to say he'll be late, one child is up in a tree, another has decided to blend chocolate cake mix in the toilet bowl, and the baby's milk is sour. Our gut reaction for this overwhelming but all too common stimuli is a piercing shriek—if we can find our voice.

Instead, take five minutes: Put dinner aside, it's been postponed anyway; the chocolate toilet bowl and sour milk can wait, but the kid up the tree can't. Later, talk to the tree-climber. Next, follow through on the toilet-bowl incident with applicable punishment (take a privilege away—something that is meaningful to the child). Above all, repeat and repeat any or all of this when necessary.

Is There Such a Thing as Detached Discipline?

I don't think so. Most discipline is an emotional reaction, and *it's okay to react emotionally.* If your child has just thrown ink all over your clean wash, you're not going to feel like asking him, "How do you *feel* about this problem?" Discipline can have emotion in it—it's unrealistic and *unreal* to expect otherwise. However, responding with feeling in a firm and consistent way is different from responding in a frazzled outburst at your wit's end. I am trying to help parents formulate a disciplinary approach that is comprehensive and that they can fall back on, so that when they respond emotionally, they also have a principle that brings continuity into the reaction. It's okay to be angry and to let your child know that. It's not okay to respond erratically and enforce measures that you later regret and retract. Whacking your child on his butt and then feeling guilty and apologizing later is not effective discipline.

The Name of the Game Is "Consequences"

Over the years I have found that the best advice I can give to parents who are struggling to develop a fair and effective means of discipline is to tell them to offer their child *consequences.* It's really simple. When you point out consequences to a child, what you're really doing is telling the child ahead of time that if such-and-such is not done, this is what's going to happen. If the consequence is something that is taken away (a privilege, a special TV program, a bike), then by not doing what he was told to do, *he—and not you—has made the choice of the consequence.* There is no guilt involved on your part; you are "out of the program." You can sit back and say, "Hey, remember, I told you. You know. You knew."

Let me hasten to add that when you offer a desirable consequence to a child for good behavior, what you're really doing is offering a bribe. A bribery is something that is offered *before* the act occurs. You say to your son, "If you rake the leaves, you can use the car." If you say, "We'd like you to finish your chores," and then when he finishes his chores, he gets to use the car—that's a reward, and there is a big difference. *Bribery is not a consequence; a reward is not a consequence*. They are three separate things, and parents need to keep them straight in their mind.

Teaching a child about consequences is a parallel learning process in which parents learn how to allow their children to learn about choosing consequences. It is never easy for parents to do this—to stand by and watch their child experience disappointment or discomfort. But that is the name of the game. In our adult life, we are constantly confronted by the consequences of the choices we make on all levels of our lives—in careers, in intimate relationships, in friendships. Why shouldn't children begin to learn about consequences at an early age? It is a way of preparing them for later life—*and* it is a fair and effective way of structuring their current experiences.

Indeed, children learn about consequences on a regular basis at school and at friends' homes. Why not also in their own home? The school regimen involves a series of consequences on several different levels. If children do well on a test, they get an "A"; the consequences of their good study habits are that they learn something and they get a good grade. On another level, if the school bell rings signalling the end of recess, but they linger outside for ten minutes, then they will receive consequences in the form of losing privileges. Kids readily learn to adapt to these circumstances in the school setting because they are consistently and firmly enforced. Kids also learn to abide by consequences when they are visiting their friends' homes. Mothers are often surprised when they hear another mother comment on how well-behaved her child was—because the mother rarely gets to experience the alleged good behavior. Why is that? Because learning to enforce consequences with one's own children is one of the hardest jobs parents face. It means *not* confusing love and discipline; it means being firm and consistent.

One of the most frequent questions parents ask me is, At what age can you begin to teach a child about consequences? My answer is, as soon as the child understands what it means to have a privilege taken away—anywhere from 1½ to two years of age. For the earlier ages, it is *the parent* who learns about the consequences of the child's behavior. When the baby first becomes mobile—when she begins to crawl—is when your first test of control begins. This is the point at which the baby can exert her will against your will. Before, when you put the baby down in one place, the chances of her touching something outside her immediate reach were slim to none. Now that the baby can crawl, however, she can act on her fascination with your stereo by crawling over to it and handling it, mauling it, or whatever. If a five-month-old breaks a favorite vase, it is the mother who pays the consequences. The baby is too young to understand the meaning of her mother's upset screech, and she is too young to grasp that she is not allowed to touch such things. Indeed, touching and exploring is her primary activity—it is what she is supposed to be doing. So the parent has to take *anticipatory action* by moving all things of value out of reach.

The consequences that you experience as a result of your baby's behavior, or the consequences that you structure as discipline for your older child, will change with each month he or she grows. Obviously the six-month old baby who cries through his mother's Thursday night Women's Group cannot be disciplined in the same way a three- or four-year-old could. With the older child, you can explain the consequences of her behavior to her and give her a choice. You can decide to give her two chances to change the behavior before acting on the discipline. You take her out into the hallway the first time and explain that if she continues to scream, you'll both have to leave. If she tests you the second time, you go out to the hallway with the same explanation. By the third outburst, you would be ready to act on your word: You take her by the hand and you leave the group. You're not dragging her out in anger; you're following through on a well thought-out approach to teaching her *consequences*.

The child who is unschooled in the realities of consequences can be downright dangerous. Several years ago, I was at a weekend barbecue given by friends. They had a two-year-old boy whom they were raising with the "permissive approach." Anything this child did was acceptable as far as his parents were concerned (as long as it didn't actually harm himself or anybody else). I had just filled my plate with spare ribs and corn cobs and was sitting on the lawn eating and talking. With my head turned in conversation with the person next to me, I didn't see it coming: Before I knew it, the little boy was standing stark naked over my plate, happily urinating all over my food. The mother was nearby, and I waited and waited for her to take some action. Chuckling in that precious way we have as proud parents she simply said, "I guess you'll have to get another plate." *I* was the one who was forced to bear the consequences of the child's unacceptable behavior—not the child himself.

That was the last time I attended any social functions given at this particular home!

One of the reasons I'm so adamant about the value of consequences as a natural means of discipline is because I have seen the effects of not being made to experience the consequences of my own irresponsibility as a child. Amazingly, I got my first inkling of a deficiency in this area at the ripe age of 45 when I got divorced. I moved into an apartment and had to take care of myself for the first time in my life. On the sixth day after moving in, I realized I didn't have any clean dishes. I put the dishes in the dishwasher and blithely added laundry soap. I left for an hour, and returned to an apartment flooded with suds. I didn't know how to wash dishes, I'd never washed my own clothes, I knew nothing about fending for myself in the kitchen. In short, I knew absolutely nothing about consequences in everyday, personal life situations. Professionally, I was skilled at foreseeing the consequences of medications, physical conditions, pediatric illnesses, parental disciplinary approaches, and on and on. But as a grown adult, I was virtually oblivious to the simplest, most basic levels of behavioral consequences.

As with our previous ingredients of discipline, there our important differences between consumed and consuming parents. The consumed parent needs to let the child begin experiencing the consequences of his actions by following through on limit-setting and not giving into the bribery urge. The consuming parent rarely allows the child to experience consequences because of the need for parental control and the high level of expectations. The child of consuming parents doesn't experience the consequences of his own behavior because the autonomy of that behavior has been so consistently structured by the parent. The child of the consumed parent doesn't experience the consequences of his own behavior because he bribes his way out of it.

I used the concept of consequences a lot with my own children. The two boys were very close to each other in age—a year and nine days apart. When they were awakened in the morning—one was always more difficult to get up than the other—*they had choices*. They got up and got ready to leave for school, or they missed school. Of course, their mother had to be prepared to put up with having the child home all day, so we were careful not make things worse for her. But, fortunately, we got quick results, because our son didn't really expect us to make him sit with his own consequences. As a dawdler, he ended up spending the entire day dealing with the consequences of having lingered in bed for a half hour, and he didn't like that at all.

If your child wants to wear green pants and a yellow polka-dot shirt to school, it's not going to take him very long to find out that the combination doesn't go well together. But if he likes it anyway, why create the problem for yourself as a parent by saying, "That looks awful." The mother doesn't have to argue with the child about what clothes to wear. Let him choose his own consequences, whenever possible.

The same principle applies for dinnertime. Dinner is probably the most embattled meal of the day. There is a very common tendency for parents to set a time for children to be home for dinner—say, six o'clock. Is it reasonable to punish the child who walks in at five past six? I don't think so. Many parents punish the lateness by scolding or sending the child to his room afterwards. But isn't it simpler to avoid the yelling and the nagging and just let the child bear the consequences of his behavior? If he comes in at five past six, dinner is still going on. If he comes in at six-fifteen, he serves himself. If he comes in past six-thirty, food is no longer being served. What is so important about everybody eating at the same time? Often, mealtime becomes a battle in which each person wants to tell everybody else what happened during the day, and no one wants to listen to anyone else. (Only on *The Waltons* did mealtimes purr along as meaningful times of family exchange.) When the children are old enough, it is easier and usually far more peaceful to leave the dinner and the clean-up to the individual, and make it a lot easier on the cook.

One of my mothers told me an amusing approach she uses to solve one aspect of dinnertime problems. If her kids have left books and clutter on the table, she simply puts all the dinner dishes on the floor and sets an area of the floor as if everyone were going to eat there. This makes her point in a dramatic way that is also somewhat humorous. Her kids invariably get the message immediately, clean the table, and set it for dinner.

Say there's a four-year-old going to pre-school and a seven-year-old going to second grade. The mother goes to work in the morning, so there is that rushed schedule. The kids sit in the kitchen, dawdling with their food. So, that's it. Fine, they don't eat. They go to school and get really hungry, so they eat their lunch at recess or try to eat during class. Then, they either get caught and disciplined, or they have no lunch left at lunch period. In other words, they encounter the *consequences* of dawdling over their food at breakfast.

When I used to play football with my friends at La Cienega park three miles from home, there were times when all we did was fool around on our bikes on our way home. So it took us a long time to get home. It didn't matter what story I fabricated to explain my lateness to my mother. I always got fed. I was old enough then that my mother should have said, "Dad and I have eaten dinner. Your dinner is on the stove." She didn't, and I never had to bear any consequences for my self-indulgent behavior. Simply stated, I was over-mothered.

Sometimes the principle of consequences is not as simple and clear a matter as the above examples suggest. In many situations, parents must go through a rather complex process of observation and evaluation to determine effective consequences in their child's life. I know this because there were times when I *didn't* observe and evaluate; when I let my children discover the consequences of their behavior without any intervention or interference on my part. And it didn't always work.

One of my sons holds the world's record at Taft High School for being tardy. When I look back on it now, I realize I didn't do anything about it at the time because my thinking was, Philip is a straight-A student anyway, so the tardiness obviously isn't affecting his grades, and any other consequences he had to find out for himself. But he didn't suffer from the consequences then—he suffered later as a young adult who discovered, to his dismay, that being irresponsible was no longer acceptable. His good grades didn't matter then—but his level of maturity did.

This is where the principle of consequences gets complex. I was letting my son experience the consequences of his behavior, but it wasn't helping to change his behavior in a positive direction. It was time for me as a parent to intervene and to attempt to structure some consequences that *would* facilitate positive change. To intervene in such a manner takes time, effort, and a lot of thought and introspection. It also takes a Herculean amount of self-control: The consequence structured by the parent can never be conceived in the emotion of anger or frustration. It is an *intervention*, and it comes from being objective and detached, being able to view the total situation, and being able to create disciplinary actions that are *constructive* rather than merely punitive.

Letting your children experience the consequences of their perpetually messy bedrooms is not likely to have fundamentally detrimental consequences on their later life. If they prefer to surround themselves in clutter, fine. Save yourself the effort of going to battle over this minor an issue, and let them wallow in the consequences of their messiness. But if they are playing with fire, and they could get burned and scarred for life—that's a consequence you don't want them to have. Fire is an obvious danger that compels parents to intervene. There is a whole continuum of behaviors, however, that net consequences that are not so easy to evaluate. My son's tardiness was one of those. It is in these gray areas, where there are no black-and-white answers, that parents will need to invest their time and energy in deciphering what is best for them and for their child.

One mother consulted me during a particularly sensitive disciplining issue. The process she and her husband went through to resolve a problem with their six-year-old son beautifully illustrates how the principles of firmness, consistency, and flexibility can co-exist in an optimal approach to fair disciplining. The experience also illustrates what I view as one of the most valuable qualities of today's young parents: the courage and willingness to engage in self-reflection. This self-reflection helped them to change their own behavior and move clearly *out* of the consuming/consumed cycle and into solid, healthy parenting. The Jamisons were willing to examine the motives beneath their rules and to include their child in the process of searching for a resolution that would reflect the child's own unique needs as well as their own. Following is a transcription of the mother's description of their experience.

"My husband and I have always been adamantly against toy guns. We had agreed that our child would not be allowed to play with guns. Period. This last

Christmas, Jeremy received a toy gun as a present from some friends of ours. He opened it while I was in another room, and when I came in and saw him already playing with it, I got very upset. I immediately called my husband at work, and we both agreed that we did not want to allow Jeremy to keep it. That night, we told him that we didn't like that sort of playing, and that he could have the gun for the next few hours but then it would be taken away.

"We did just that and then, of course, it promptly became a big obsession with him. Every time he got a present he said, 'Maybe it's the gun.' Everything he had became a gun—sandwiches, a salt shaker, a broken toy. We bought him a small golf cart and he took the handle off and turned it into a gun!

"About the same time, his teacher reported that he had become somewhat antisocial in school. She had observed that Jeremy didn't seem able to participate in playing with the other boys. Most kids, we were told, were busy reenacting this and that villain or hero from TV, but Jeremy usually stood on the sidelines. We told the teacher that we did not allow television because we did not like the violent quality that seemed to dominate many children's programs. The teacher then suggested that Jeremy would do better if he also had these TV characters to relate to and share with the other boys.

"We decided to let Jeremy watch his first television show. Within a few days of this change, however, every game he played became this violent superhero-action scenario. Our child seemed to be saturated by everything we were repulsed by. We did a lot of talking between ourselves, with the teacher, and with Jeremy. The teacher told me that in her impression, Jeremy was feeling guilty for playing these games that most kids were playing. From his perspective, he was just being normal, but he knew that Mommy was very uncomfortable with his behavior and he felt that he was being 'bad'."

"The very next day we left on a camping trip for ten days. After the first two or three days, Jeremy's behavior became totally out-of-control. We couldn't believe the change! He was fighting us every step of the way. We had never encountered such belligerent, contentious behavior in him. In fact, Jeremy had been an exceptionally even-tempered child, so the change was even more dramatic for us.

"Finally, we decided to have a family meeting. We began by having each of us say what we wanted to change in one another. Jeremy wanted Mommy and Daddy not to be angry with him when he played games we didn't approve of. My husband and I wanted Jeremy to be more cooperative in his behavior instead of acting out his frustrations. In turn, we would play his games with him. We even gave his gun back to him at this point. Instead of judging him, I decided I would participate in his play to a limited extent. When I was tired of playing the game, I would suggest something else.

"This approach was the beginning of a whole new child. We have more togetherness; we let him watch TV an hour a day, and during that hour he rarely watches the violent shows anymore; and he plays with his gun sometimes, but it's not as important as it used to be.

"In short, we stopped judging him and trusted that he wasn't going to grow up to be a killer just because he played with toy guns on occasion. We learned that we couldn't just enforce our values on Jeremy and expect him to adjust. Not being able to share in a big chunk of the world that was common to his classmates was hurting Jeremy, and we needed to hear that. We realized it was perfectly normal for him to want to play with guns and to act out various TV characters with the other kids. We had to re-evaluate our position; we had to take

Jeremy's feelings and needs into consideration in order to reach a compromise that we could all live with."

Each major discipline issue is complex and unique. As parents, you can only begin from the perspective of your own values and beliefs, as the Jamisons did. If you are uncomfortable with your child having a toy gun, then you cannot allow yourself to say, "Well, everybody in the neighborhood has a gun, so I have to let my child have one, too." It is essential that you communicate your true feelings and values to your child. Then, you wait and see. The Jamisons let their child know, and it didn't work. So they counterflexed—they re-examined and re-evaluated—and they compromised, *but with limits.*

This family's experience highlights an important but overlooked component of effective discipline: teaching your children how to express themselves. Self-expression is a kind of preventative medicine in a family, because it keeps the air clearer of tension and resentments. The best way I know to teach kids how to communicate is by doing it ourselves—with our spouses and with our children. *We* have to learn how *not* to give mixed messages before we can expect our kids to be straight with us. We also have to "practice what we preach"—to live by what we tell our children.

One of my mother's told me how her 13-year-old son spontaneously offered her the admonition, "Now, Mom, don't let anyone make you do something you don't want to do." She had been stressed and anxious over a problem at work, and her son had counseled her with a principle she had expressed to him countless times.

Parents need to model clear communication by taking the time to be in touch with their own feelings and responses. So many of us grew up with parents who did not know how to say what they felt, or who believed it was un-adult to do so. Sooner or later the feelings would erupt in outbursts and flared tempers, or the walls of silence and distance would grow even thicker. The black-and-white polarities that characterized our parent's generation in the area of discipline also characterized it in the area of self-expression and communication. Yesterday's parents were in a fixed role as authoritarians and providers. Today's parents view themselves in a far more fluid role in which they are also vulnerable human beings who can give *and* receive comfort and support.

The Bottom Line

When parents are able to establish firm and consistent discipline in the context of consequences, it becomes part of the fabric of the parent-child relationship—part of their ongoing pattern of communication. The bottom line is, *we are all subject to limits and we are all subject to the consequences of our behavior.* Why should parents have to wake up every day with a sense of dread, wondering how many arguments they are going to have with their kids or how many crises are going to erupt? Why should parents heave themselves into chairs each night with a prayerful groan, "Thank God, I made it through another day." Why should every mealtime be a battleground? Why should every bath be a hassle? Why should household chores require endless nagging? Worse, why should each year bring a whole new set of behavior problems and developmental crises that leave parents feeling as if they are back in Square One? Unfortunately, this is the case for many parents simply by virtue of the fact that they are parents and their kids are kids. But *it doesn't have to be that way.*

The approach to discipline described in this chapter requires that you use observation and self-reflection to get the larger picture of your interactions with your child. It also requires that you be *present* for your child; you have to stop and take the time to pay attention to exactly what is going on. In the beginning, you have to stay in touch with your child's behavior all the time in order to initiate your changes. But in the long run, if you do this at an early age, you'll have a lot more time for yourself with a lot less aggravation and frustration. And that's the whole point from a parent's perspective.

To be firm and consistent with the eight- or ten-month-old who is constantly touching things requires that you put in time. The younger child doesn't comprehend yet, so you have to actually take the child away from whatever he's touching, or remove the object itself. Parents often make the mistake of thinking that by screaming often enough, the child will stop the undesired behavior. But many times the "No" just means attention to the child—another way of saying, "Hey, look what I'm doing now." There have already been 300 no's that day, so how does he differentiate? He's already heard, "No, you can't spit....No, you can't throw your food on the floor....No, you can't grab my earring.... No, you can't pee on the floor." There are a million things he's heard no for, and he's ignored most of them. And there hasn't been one yes, so when he goes over to touch the stereo, your "no" is like water off a duck's back. To be effective with a child this age, you have to stop what you're doing and remove him from the area.

Even by the time the child is two, it still takes time and effort to convince him to stop doing something that he is enjoying doing. By the time he is five, however, he has learned to respond to your first request. And if this isn't the case—if you end up telling him to do or not do something 10 times, then it's because you haven't set limits from the beginning and you have lost control.

It is all too easy for most of us as parents to end up red-faced, frustrated and shouting—and that's what constitutes discipline in the household. "Go to your room....Clean up that mess....Get out of my sight!"— the discipline becomes the end result of emotions and reactions that are out-of-control in the parent. My point is simply that you can teach limit-setting to your child in a way that causes *you* far less grief.

There is the child who says he is starving. Then he takes two bites and says he's through and spends the rest of the time playing with his food. And you sit there, frustrated for a half hour, trying to get him to eat. What are you teaching him when you do that? You're not teaching him anything—except, perhaps, that he can keep you at the table interminably and still not eat! However, you would be teaching him something useful if you told him that he could leave the table but that there would be no food later. If he knows ahead of time that there isn't going to be any food available later, and he still chooses to leave the table, then *he* has made the decision, and *he* is learning how to set his own limits and to live with the consequences.

The process that you as parents go through to create limits and enforce discipline in your child's life is a complex one in which you have to be in touch with the child's unique personality and needs. In short, you have to know your child *before* you enforce something consistently and firmly.

Here, parents are truly the only experts. We "experts" can cite a million examples illustrating a million different facets of discipline situations. Yet the all-important fact remains that we are not in your particular situation, in your particular time and place, and we are not talking about *your* child. That is why, ultimately, your intuition must have the deciding vote. If you use a little of me, or a little of another expert, *plus your intuition*, you'll do fine. But only as long as you include your own intuition. Follow me verbatim, or follow someone else verbatim, without the compass of your own "gut" feelings, and it's not going to work.

If I were to give a "final" word of "advice" to parents on the subject of discipline, it would be to *remember that you're people before you're parents.* Think of the things that give you happiness that *are not* related to your child. And know that if you take the time to do those things for yourself, then it's going to be a lot easier for you to control your child in a way that is truly healthy for both of you. If you are unhappy, if you are too tied down, it makes the disciplining and the controlling all that much harder—*and* it makes both you and your child more vulnerable to abuse.

A mother who has been in the house from six in the morning until nine that night with a three-month-old infant who has cried all day long is not going to feel good about herself for very long. One of my most frequent admonitions to my mothers is, "Think about yourself and *do something* for yourself." None of the approaches I have described in this chapter will be effective if they are executed by a chronically hassled and over-wrought parent. "Think about yourself" is therefore as important a "rule" as is "Be firm and consistent in your discipline." Thinking about yourself ensures that *your* individuality will not be sacrificed. It also helps to ensure that you will not compromise the fragile individuality that is emerging, day by day, in your child.

℞

Prescriptions for Winning at Discipline

FOR EVERYONE

1. Trust your own feelings and intuitions.
2. Learn that it's okay for your kids to *not like* you once in a while, and it's okay for you to *not like* your kids once in a while.
3. Learn to distinguish between types of manipulative behavior.
4. Believe in your own parenting expertise and know that you are doing the best you can.
5. Use the principles of *consistency, firmness,* and *consequences* as the foundation of your disciplinary actions.
6. At all cost, present a "united front" on discipline issues.

FOR THE CONSUMED PARENT

1. At all cost, avoid bribing your child.
2. At all cost, avoid reinforcing manipulative behavior through hesitancy and indecision. (Keep the "Fairytale Nightmare" a fairytale.)
3. Remember that *you* are the teacher.
4. Stay strong in the face of your child's natural tendency to *test limits.*
5. Learn to say "NO" in a voice that is firm and free of doubt.

FOR THE CONSUMING PARENT

1. Learn to *teach* rather than enforce discipline.

2. Decide what your essential limits are and learn to negotiate and compromise.
3. Find ways to say "YES" to your child.
4. Learn to say *no* in a voice that is firm but free of condemnation.
5. Be willing to listen to your child's input.
6. Be willing to be *wrong*.

5 ❦

Midnight
Marauders

Sleep is a unique pattern that your baby learns to do on a habitual basis. Remember that crying is as normal as testing. It is a form of preverbal communication and does not necessarily signal distress.

Parents ask, "Where does the consuming/consumed cycle *begin*?" My answer is, it begins with sleep!

Among all the problematic events of childhood, there are few for which parents are less prepared and more inclined toward mismanagement than the sleep problem. Babies and children continually test us and their environment—and such behavior is completely normal. When the baby begins to test her limits at night when the rest of the household wants to sleep, we label it a "sleep problem." Bedtime and middle-of-the-night testing take place when parents are at their most vulnerable—when the day of sharing has turned into the longer day of tyranny, and when they are too weary to regard the crying as another opportunity to face the challenge of teaching limits to the baby.

Sleep problems begin when parents have expectations that they will have their nine-month-old in bed by 7 P.M. The infant doesn't know to stop testing his environment just because his parents are exhausted from a day full of work, mealtime, playtime, bath time, and dinner dishes. *Between nine months to one year of age, the infant begins to extend his curiosity about life and its limitations into the time grownups usually set aside for sleep.* Sleeping at certain times is a habit; baby is just beginning to develop this habit, while mother and father already have it down pat.

Around 7 or 8 P.M., you feel as if the day will never end, and each cry or fall sounds like a stampede of wild buffalo—and the buffalo aren't tired! Then follows the endless time it takes to get the child to bed...get out of bed for a cookie...back into bed...get out of bed for a glass of milk...back into bed...get out of bed to go to the potty...and on and on. Mary Poppins, where are you???

How does this nightmare begin?

It could begin with the healthy, strong, cute nine-month-old who has been broken from a night bottle for six months. Suddenly, he's up and screaming one night at 2:30 A.M. Father is thrashing through the pages of Dr. Spock and waiting for the pediatrician to come on the line, while Mother is holding and rocking the baby—who is now smiling, and what do you know—uttering his very first intelligible word. When uncomfortable clothing, middle-ear infections, or appendicitis have been ruled out as the cause of crying, from out of nowhere comes the idea that a bottle *just this once* won't hurt. After all, didn't he just say *Da Da*? By this time it's 3:00 A.M., and you're much too bleary-eyed to realize that you've started something that should stop now!

The same thing happens the following night, because it took the infant screamer a hot second to figure out (in a baby sort of way) that this is the time when both parents are home, willing, and too tired to weigh the consequences—a great time to take advantage. No need to phone the pediatrician or consult Spock this time. Just a bottle, a precious smile, and two zombie-like parents who are beginning to stomp around and mutter a lot to each other.

One week later the same routine is still occurring with one exception—the screamer is playing with the bottle instead of drinking it. Now you are not only stomping and muttering, but swearing as well.

The screamer is now fifteen months old and has discovered her "long nap" at night is interfering with all the action. Now she gets up between 11 P.M. and midnight, so that you barely get your eyes closed. Since in the last few months her understanding has expanded along with her vocabulary, her requests are more sophisticated and numerous: cookies, toast, raisins, bagels. And you comply: anything to get the star of this unsolicited "late show" to turn herself off. Paradoxically, at this age there is a decrease in appetite—although it mysteriously reappears during late night hours. Since anxious parents have the impression baby is "barely surviving" from one meal to the next, they jump at the opportunity to get every morsel they can into her—no matter what the hour. By this time, Father is blaming Mother and Mother is blaming Father.

Our screamer is now age two to 28 months and is in a junior bed. But even if she's still in the crib, she has become the resident decathlon champion, vaulting from her crib to your room with great dexterity. Now she doesn't have to cry to signal her nightly assault—as you soon find out one midnight while the two of you are making love, and a tiny but insistent voice, no more than two feet away from you, asks for milk and cookies. What a climax to a climax—or is it *"cookies interruptus"*!

Is this the same adorable nine-month-old? Now all you want to do is tie her down, weighted to a ball and chain, with a few thumb tacks sprinkled outside her door for good measure.

Before her third birthday, she will discover that going to bed is a complete waste of time. You may have established 7:30 P.M. as bedtime, but to her it's cookie time, story time, water time, and (this is the clincher), potty time. At this stage, you are probably hung-up about her potty training, so how can you allow an opportunity like this to slip by? The potty trip alone is worth at least 40 minutes because "she really has to go." It's now 9:00 P.M. and quiet, but come 10:00 P.M. and guess who? Now she *"really* has to go" and could she please have a cookie—after all, it's a big event.

It's not too difficult to see what has happened to your life—what's left of it. You not only have a full-fledged midnight marauder on your hands, but the entire household is being victimized by sleep pollution. What started as a singular incident of interrupted sleep has now evolved into a chronic problem of *not* sleeping. From this stage of nocturnal bedlam evolves the too-tired preschooler who resists nursery school with a vengeance. Never have you seen her so cross and mean. She may become a nursery school drop-out simply because she is unable to function on five or six hours of uninterrupted sleep.

The specter of being the perfect parent teeters on the point of devastation once a crying baby has dominated your night. You feel panic rise within you as all your "buttons" of insecurity are exposed and activated by the wailing sounds of this fragile, totally helpless baby. In Chapter 3 we heard from the mother who spent the first five months of her new motherhood desperately trying to cope with her baby's crying. Hunter actually fared better at night than during the day, but her experiences with dealing with his chronic crying are very similar to what parents of midnight criers experience. Mary continues her story:

"It took me a long time to realize that Hunter's cries didn't necessarily mean he wanted to be held. I had spent most of my days holding and rocking him, forcing myself to put him down for brief periods, but not being able to tolerate the cries for more than five minutes. My inner struggle with this was agonizing—I felt constantly *pulled*. You [Dr. Zukow] had been telling me all along, 'Let him cry, Mary. Put him down. Don't hold him every time he cries.' But I just *couldn't* bring myself to ignore the crying.

"At about the third month, my mother-in-law arrived for a visit—and, oh, did she defy the stereotype of her title! I was never so glad for the presence of one person in all my life. She didn't judge me—or the baby. She just quietly made suggestions and demonstrated, unobtrusively, how to do things differently.

"One day about mid-morning Hunter was crying again. He had stopped long enough to be breastfed, and then the moment he finished, up came the wail. I began to rock him. My mother-in-law said, 'Mary, why don't you put him down? He's tired, he's sleepy, he's just been fed. Try putting him down.'

"I told her flat out that I just couldn't do that—he cries when I put him down and I just have to pick him up again.

"She asked my permission to try. I gave it! She took Hunter and placed him in his stroller—the kind that turns into a 'bassinet on wheels'—and gave it a couple of rocks. Hunter was sound asleep in five minutes! I was dumbfounded.

"I tried her approach several times while she was visiting, and with the help of her presence, I was able to let Hunter cry. The moment she left I folded in half and felt like I was back at Square One. But I did have something to fall back on—it had worked when my mother-in-law was here, and I would have to make it work again.

"I literally *assigned* myself the task of putting Hunter down when he cried and building up my tolerance to the sounds of his distress. My maximum was 15 minutes—and I sweat out each and every minute. I never did excel at tuning out his cries. My husband was much better at that. He seemed to have a basic trust that everything was okay, whereas I had a basic sense of *panic* that I was failing my mission as Mother. Looking back, I understand all of the psychology of it, and even with that understanding, I'm amazed I survived."

Sleep problems and the crying that inevitably accompanies them often inaugurate the consumed/consuming cycle of parenting. When Mary first brought her baby home from the hospital, she wasn't a consumed parent. It was a behavior pattern that she developed as a result of this crucial first encounter with manipulative behavior. The root assumptions about parenting mentioned earlier, coupled with Mary's basic personality characteristics, sent her down the consumed path. Another parent with different assumptions and a different combination of personality qualities might turn onto the consuming pathway. The parent about to veer off onto the consumed pathway inwardly develops an attitude of fear and intimidation, and moves into the defensive mode. The parent on the path of consuming behavior also feels fear, but the personality style of reaction is more one of taking control and handling as many variables as possible to control the baby's crying.

WHEN IT COMES TO THE ISSUE OF YOUR BABY CRYING, EVERY PARENT GETS CONSUMED. Differences will emerge in what parents are willing and unwilling to try. The consumed parent is usually unwilling to try anything but being completely attentive to the crying child; the consuming parent is more willing to try techniques.

Both groups of parents share a sometimes disabling fear of responding in the "wrong" way and harming the baby.

Bedtime Bribery—Banish It!

We teach our children how to manipulate us and plunk ourselves on the consumed path of parenting the moment we make bedtime a bargain. The more often that bribery is offered, the less often the child is willing to sleep on his own. His desire now becomes one of keeping you on the hook to see how far he can pull you and in how many directions. Sleeping, like food, becomes something he knows you are anxious for him to do. When you make a huge issue out of sleeping, you typically hear the following statements from the forever-testing child: "If I make potty, can I sleep in your bed?"; "If I go to bed now, can I have a cookie first?" The list is endless—and so are your nights. Unless you interrupt this pattern, *manipulation*, rather than sleep, becomes the child's habit!

Sleep is a Personal Habit

Speaking of habits, *sleep, like eating, is a habit born out of need*. As with most needs, it is manifested in totally individual ways, with some children surviving on four to six hours while others require eight to ten. I often feel that adults who sleep very long hours (10 or more) do so as a way of avoiding the day ahead. Looking at this from a child's vantage point, one sees that sleeping, even though it is needed, interferes with all the fun, playing, and stimulation of being alive and awake in the world.

Of course, you can't let a child stay up all night. But the child who cannot settle down to sleep night after night—after you've threatened, bribed, cajoled and torn your hair out—*may be trying to tell you that his bedtime is too early*. Since children have varying nap and sleep requirements, it is essential that parents first learn to determine what their child's needs are. If we look closely, we'll discover that many of these requirements are imposed by us, the adults, irrespective of the needs of the child, because that is what we have read or heard.

The example of the 2 A.M. screamer demonstrates how giving in with a bottle only allows parents to fulfill their own need to have everyone quiet down and go back to sleep. It does not allow parents to solve the problem. Unless a meal was skipped, an infant does not need a middle-of-the-night feeding. *By indulging the screamer, the parents deny her the opportunity to learn about appropriateness of demands, timing, and limits.*

The consuming parent tends to be more rigid in setting sleep times and, therefore, is somewhat less open to being manipulated. The consumed parent tends to be completely vulnerable to the baby's ever-changing feelings about sleep and when to do it. Both parents will suffer equally, however, when the baby adds ear-splitting screaming to the sleep equation.

A Few Tricks of the Tirades

Most parents ask how to tell if the crying nine-to-twelve-month-old is really in distress or just testing. How can you tell if he has been awakened by gas as a result of something he ate (or was given to "overeat"), is teething, has cramps in arms or legs, is constipated, or something more serious such as a middle-ear infection? (I always find it hard to believe that the symptoms of gas or teething only occur in the early morning hours!)

As parents grow accustomed to their baby's crying, they rapidly learn to distinguish between types of cries. The aware mother can easily tell the difference between a cry of hunger, a cry for attention, a cry of pain. However, those discriminatory abilities seem to wane in the vulnerable nighttime hours. Hence, many a parent has created a crying monster out of needless concern for the child's well-being.

It is easy to initially determine if clothing is too constrictive. Further, if the baby responds with a smile to being held after a very short time (a few minutes), medical problems probably can be ruled out for the time being—especially if there have been no recent changes in appetite, no obvious cold symptoms, and the prior day was spent in good spirits.

For the baby in pain, however, holding, rocking, and walking seldom help. A baby with a middle-ear infection (which is by far the most common cause of middle-of-the-night outbursts) will continue to cry no matter how long you hold him. This type of crying may be a signal for you to call your pediatrician. The manipulative baby is the one who has gotten the better of you: She has a big smile on her face the minute you pick her up, and she is ready to play. It takes a really strong parent to pass up that smile—especially a father who hasn't seen the baby all day long and who is thrilled to have the ability to still his baby's cries.

Once all medical problems have been ruled out and you still have a midnight screamer, your follow-up has to be quick: back to bed and allowed to cry. You must allow the baby to cry himself back to sleep, even if this pattern takes one to three weeks to break. (The 14- to 16-month-old can cry every night for a month if necessary.) Medication for this problem is often useless because it doesn't last long enough.

This issue of letting safe, comfortable, healthy babies cry themselves back to sleep at night is a controversial one. All of us "experts" have our own opinions. Some, such as "Dr. Mom," advocate going to the baby immediately and holding it. She contends that "this period [of night waking] is temporary and indicative of his developmental phase, not a permanent behavior." My experience has shown me that the opposite is true; that the behavior of night crying can become quite permanent when it is overindulged by worried parents.

Parents—particularly new ones—always assume that a crying baby is in distress. Actually, though, this is not necessarily true. *Crying is one of the baby's major forms of communication,* and it is the one to which parents inevitably respond. The baby quickly learns that crying can bring him certain benefits...juice, milk, cookies, hugs and kisses, and lots of attention. *Attention* is a big draw. Babies never give up wanting attention, once they get it. There seems to be a gene in all of us labeled MORE, and babies are quite vocal about expressing it.

I had one couple whose baby had had several severe ear infections early on, and had been hospitalized on two occasions. Needless to say, the parents were completely "gun-shy" about her crying from the beginning. Even after she was well, their first thought at the sound of a cry was, "Something dreadful is wrong again." What was interesting was that the baby learned to sound sick after she was well as a way of getting the attention she wanted. Because of the baby's early, frightening illnesses, the parents had become completely "devoted to her"—and also *consumed* by her—and gave her 100% of their time, effort, and energy. Well after the crises had passed, the entire household, day and night, was still being dictated by the cries, whimpers, and giggles of this baby. Finally, the parents reached such a state of desperation—*none* of their own needs were getting met in the slightest—that they found the courage to begin letting her cry. After a week or two, they became convinced that she really was well, and she really did need to learn some limits. Now they have a greater portion of their lives back, and their young daughter has learned an extremely important lesson.

When you bring your newborn home from the hospital, she is not *manipulative* and she has not *been manipulated*. You both start with a clean slate. Then enter the first major challenge between you—the baptism of parenthood—in the form of sleep and crying behaviors. Your interactions with your baby at these times is crucial and becomes a blueprint for your continuing patterns of parenting.

As parents, you have to make a decision. Are you willing and able to give your baby round-the-clock attention? If you're not, then you have to find ways to begin setting and teaching limits. You will find that at some point, you draw the line. And you want to start now, because this is when you have the most influence.

Crying is as normal as testing. In the previous chapter on discipline, I talked about how testing happens continually throughout childhood and how the consumed parent often winds up a slave to the child, the master manipulator. That same message applies in this chapter: *Crying can be used manipulatively; it does not necessarily mean the baby or child is unhappy*. You use your common sense, your gut feeling, and your own checklist to determine the meaning of the behavior. If the child is unhappy and crying at night, and unhappy during the day, too, then you've got to focus on what the child is unhappy with: You rule out the organic, then you look at the nursery school, then you look at the babysitter. Once you've ruled out all such factors, you know that this baby is unhappy just at night: he takes a "night-nap," and then he's very well rested and he's up to play games with you. It's as simple as that.

What *isn't* simple is actually listening to your baby cry at night. Even though you're certain she is fine and wanting to play, the sound of the crying inevitably brings anguish to any parent. I say the same thing to each parent with whom I talk: "It's a lot easier for me to tell you to allow your baby to cry than it is for you to sit there and *listen* to your baby crying." One mother asked me how long she should allow her baby to cry. I said, "As long as you can stand it." Then jokingly I added, "If you feel the baby is crying too loudly, call me." Several days later my phone rang at 3:00 A.M. I groggily answered and was blasted by the robust cries of her nine-month-old. The mother was angry and frustrated and she wanted me to know what she was going through. A year later we were able to laugh about it because by then, her baby had learned to sleep through the night.

Another mother had just finished nursing her baby through a painful ear infection. During that time, the baby's cries had been immediately responded to. Once he was well, he just didn't want to go to sleep at night and continued his pattern of crying, expecting the same immediate response. The parents had already been through one round with night crying, and so as hard as it was, they decided to hold firm on this second round. The first night he cried for 3 ½ hours; the second night he cried for a half hour; and the third night he cried for 30 seconds. After that, it never happened again. Babies and parents both have to get through that first night or two.

Having said all this, let me hasten to add that if it's okay with you to be up all night long, that's fine. I'm not saying that it's *not* fine; I'm only attempting to help the parent who finds it stressful and exhausting to be up all night.

Let me also reiterate one of my main points in the previous chapter on discipline: Parents have to be aware of what fits for them when they are laying down rules. If I tell parents to let their baby cry at night, but they overreact and overcompensate with the baby out of their own discomfort, then they will have done exactly the antithesis of what we are hoping to do—which is raise a healthy, independent, non-manipulative child.

The bottom line is always, "Go with what feels the most right to you." My only addendum to this "rule" would be: Make sure you're including your own needs as a person when you evaluate these various methods of dealing with childhood problems—because if you choose in favor of the baby's needs but at the exclusion of your own, your baby will ultimately get the backlash in one form or another.

Physical Restrictions. Physically restricting toddlers

and midnight marauders who are sufficiently mobile to climb out of their cribs or beds and wander off in search of you is *not* cruel—just a reasonable demonstration of the limits you set for this type of behavior. Consuming parents are more open to these methods because they are more comfortable with taking control; consumed parents tend to lose all color from their face and shake their heads "no." Believing that it is bad or detrimental to take control, the consumed parent is initially shocked by any method that establishes an absolute limit for the child. However, their shock slowly fades in direct proportion to their exhaustion and desperation. Eventually, many of my consumed parents have given these methods a try—and been deeply reassured by the positive results.

For the decathlon champion, I suggest a volleyball net over the crib. Don't feel guilty. He knows what he's been doing and he'll know what you're doing—which is demonstrating that his antics can't continue along this line. I learned about this approach during my residency training. As soon as the sick kids in cribs began to feel better, they would try to crawl out at night. To protect them, we put a net over their cribs. Now there isn't a hospital crib in the whole country that doesn't have some kind of protection over the top so that the kids can't crawl out once they are well.

Another method of restricting the older toddler is attaching a slippery plastic doorknob to the inside of his bedroom door (available at children's and hardware stores). When the child knocks and kicks against the door, which he undoubtedly will, you are instantly informed of the fact that he is down on the floor and not in bed. What you are informing *him* by your healthy action of benign neglect is that you are standing firm on what you believe—that he should remain in his room until morning, even if he falls asleep on the floor. (He won't catch cold, and you can sneak in later to cover him, not move him!) You're also teaching him that he cannot manipulate you with loud noises, kicking, unnecessary pleas, or flaming re-entries.

If the idea of physically restricting your marauding child brings chills to your spine and a lump to your throat, consider the following scenario which I have heard countless times from *very* frustrated parents.

You go to bed at 11 P.M. and by 11:30 you have entered your deepest period of sleep. At 12:30 your three-year-old toddles in, tugs at your sheets (and at your hair), jolts you out of your peaceful reveries and says sweetly, "Can I sleep with you?"

Perhaps the first couple of nights you say no, but she cries and cries, so you go fetch her and bring her into bed with you. On the third night, there is no crying prelude—she simply toddles in at the hour of her choice and crawls into bed with you. A few hours later, say at 4 A.M., you roll over and there's a nice, toasty little body. You have a whole day of work ahead of you and you need your sleep, so you let her sleep on.

On the fourth night, your sweet, cute three-year-old adds yet another element to her nightly marauding routine: a request for a cookie. Now she wakes you up, *gets* you up to get her food, and then goes back into bed with you. By this stage of the marauding process, your child has managed to gain dominion over your cherished nighttime hours, so that you have the uneasy feeling each night as you slip under the covers that you have no control over how the night will go. Will you be allowed to sleep comfortably entwined in your spouse's arms until daybreak? Or will you be invaded by your resident midnight marauder? Only your child knows for sure! And God forbid you should get the urge to make love spontaneously in the middle of the night. Are you alone? Will you be left alone? Many couples I've worked with have not-so-hilarious stories to tell about the night their three- or four-year-old walked in on them in the middle of lovemaking. To put it mildly, the experience cramped their actions for some time to come.

I think these night hours are the most vulnerable time for parents, and it is the time when they are the most easily manipulated by their children. Any way that you handle it—short of giving in to it—causes you lost sleep.

If you say no and groggily tell the child to go back to bed, she is likely to throw a fit right there and then, and so you have to get up anyway and *take* her back to her bed. If you use either restrictive method I've suggested, you will probably have to suffer through a few bumpy nights of protest before the child learns that her demanding behavior cannot win you over.

As with all the other disciplining issues we've discussed, I am offering methods of intervention that are applicable to children who are *not* attempting to express a serious problem. Fighting parents, a bully in the preschool, learning problems, and so forth, can all trigger the type of nighttime behavior I have described. In such cases, it may or may not be appropriate to use restrictive methods in conjunction with your sensitive and caring probing of the underlying problem. However, *nighttime marauding behavior is in itself a perfectly natural phase of exploration and testing for the growing child*, and it may arise to plague you for no deeper reason than your child is either raring to go at 3:00 A.M., or likes to cuddle in the big bed between Mommy and Daddy. Even if the behavior is a message from your child that she wants/needs more attention or affection, find a way to give her more *at an appropriate time*. If you give in out of guilt in the wee hours of the night, you will also be placing yourself in a consumed pattern of parenting that will have repercussions 24 hours a day.

My suggestions for restricting the overly mobile child during the night are in response to the many haggard and exhausted parents who have come to me for solutions. Most parents I know lead extremely hectic lives in which the loss of sleep adds yet another, highly stressful variable. Under such conditions, the chance of slipping into abusive behavior increases dramatically. Then what we've got is the vicious cycle of abuse in which the parent is, in essence, abused by the child's demanding, manipulative behavior during the night, and then the child gets abused by the parent's frenzied fits during the day.

I have seen many sensitive, loving parents resort to restriction as a last ditch effort to salvage their nighttime peace of mind. To their surprise the method worked, and rather than leaving them feeling like the World's Meanest Parents, left them refreshed for the next day of creative and sane parenting. It restored their sense of control, it taught their children healthy nighttime sleep habits, and it gave them back their space, their privacy, and their intimacy.

Physically restricting the disruptive child is simply an alternative to verbal limit-setting. Words are not the only way to communicate with your child. Real communication is the art of demonstrating your position on a given issue, whether via words or actions. Limits, both verbal and physical, are lessons in life, and if you don't provide them—who will?

Bedtime—
Nothing Is Certain But Change

A child's needs will most always determine at what hour the appropriate bedtime is set. As the child grows older (eight years and up), the actual hour will be later and later as the need arises: increase in homework, participation in sports, more demanding social life. Keep yourself outside the reach of the consumed/consuming cycle of parenting and teach this older child self-realization by allowing him the bedtime of his choice, *but don't let his choice influence the time he must arise in the morning.* This is harder for consuming parents because they experience it is a loosening of control. My point is, by adapting to the child's real needs, you stand a much better chance of evoking the desired behavior and remaining in control. The child who learns that going to bed at an unreasonable hour hampers getting up the next day is learning *consequences* which continue to shape his developing maturity. If children are initially made responsible for their own physical needs without having to adhere blindly to parental requirements, they will learn what the requirements are for their own unique being. This is the gift of *self-awareness*—the freedom and space to discover who they *are* and who they *are not*.

The Nap—For You Or Baby?

Consuming parents are more likely to insist on naps at rigidly enforced times of the day, while consumed parents will tend to be caught in the web of the child dictating up and down times. Both parents are coming from opposite ends of the continuum to the center balance point (hopefully) of learning to observe the child's behavior, determining what needs fit the child, and then enforcing limits that reflect these observations.

My opinion is that napping is an individual need of the toddler; school-age children usually do not require naps. The earlier you recognize that the child is ready to give up napping, the better for everyone. Also recognize that if it is *you* who needs the time way from baby, by all means, take your well-deserved time, but do not require a child who is not sleepy to sleep. This is a waste of time and energy, and is inconsiderate of the child's individual sleep requirements. Resting in his room, reading, or playing with quiet toys is just as effective as a nap.

The child who sleeps a lot during the day is probably doing it from boredom. (Any possible organic cause, such as low iron, can be checked out by your physician.) Although the aware parent can eliminate boredom to some degree, the tolerance for boredom is as individual a trait as is a child's sleep requirements, and for the most part, must be allowed and accepted as part of that child's personality.

Nightmares

Most children outgrow nightmares by the age of five and thereafter have only occasional ones, which are mostly related to new school situations, new houses, or new babies. For children under five, most nightmares occur shortly after sleep and before midnight. There is a non-narcotic medication for the child with early nightmares that can lessen their intensity as well as the child's reactions to them. The use of medication to deal with this problem is controversial. I am comfortable with *trying* it, but when it loses its efficacy, you have to search for different answers. When you've eliminated all the common things such as television programs, certain comic books, certain holidays (like Halloween), certain movies, the child might be developing a real phobic response and it's time to consult with a child psychologist. The child who has serious emotional reactions as a result of a family tragedy, divorce, or physical trauma also may need short-term psychotherapy.

Usually, parents can readily identify a nightmare cry and respond by giving comfort in whatever way is appropriate. Once the crying has stopped, however, the child should be put back down for sleep. Nightmares can easily precipitate a sleep problem because they instigate a pattern of the child being awakened in the middle of the night, the parent having to respond, and then the child being put back to sleep—or worse, being brought into the parents' bed.

Cardinal rule: DO NOT BRING YOUR CRYING BABY INTO YOUR BED. Wake her, which might be difficult to do as she sobs and thrashes about. Don't give her cookies, don't haul her out to the VCR room. Hold her for a few minutes in *her* room, make sure her night-light is on, speak reassuringly, even put on soothing music in *her* room and put her back to bed. Think of it like putting your child back on the horse after she's just fallen off, or helping her up from her first fall on the ice to try again.

My son Carlos had awful nightmares two to three times a week. His screams would pierce through the house. I would wake straight up, sure that somebody had just attacked him in his crib. It was truly bloodcurdling. But we still did not bring him into our bed. Each time it happened, one of us acted consistently by going immediately to his room, picking him up and cradling him for a few minutes, and then putting him back in his crib. The behavior did not accelerate into manipulation. After about six months the nightmares abated, and we weren't left with a child who now believed he could wake us up at any point during the night, cry, and get what he wanted.

In recognizing that the nighttime crying is in response to a nightmare and is not a manipulative maneuver on the child's part, the parent must still maintain firmness and consistency in putting the child back to bed and then disengaging. Because a baby's cries in response to a nightmare can sound so terrifying, it is easy to foster a night-waking pattern so that any time the child wakes up, he knows he can cry and his parent or parents will come to him.

Sometimes parents will interpret night crying as being due to nightmares when, in fact, it is due to something altogether different. I had a 3½-year-old niece who was waking up screaming at ten or eleven every night. We assumed it was due to nightmares. One night I was over for dinner and at 11 o'clock she started screaming. I went in with her parents; she was awake and we comforted her. I happened to sit down on her bed and I noticed that the hallway night-light was casting a shadow of a giant rooster on the wall. The actual rooster, which had a plant growing out of it, was positioned on the child's bureau; it had been a recent present. The angle at which the night-light was hitting the rooster made its shadow loom ominously across the entire wall. My little niece would awaken from whatever dream she was having, see that shape, and start screaming. We took away the rooster and she never again had a "nightmare."

Responding to nighttime crying in a way that does *not* foster a nighttime crying pattern is one of the hardest things for a parent to do. Our babies are more vulnerable in the middle of the night, and so are we. It can be anguishing to put your child back to bed, turn out the light, and leave the room even as he or she continues to wail. However, try to keep in mind the long-range view of the consequences you may be engendering by over-responding to nighttime crying. In the larger picture you do not want to saddle either yourself or your child with an enduring sleep problem. With this in mind, you can surround your child with a sense of security and comfort while, at the same time, setting limits.

Examining the Controversy

I realize that my approaches to discipline and sleep problems may seem "hard line" and therefore controversial. In a recent issue of the magazine, *Contemporary Pediatrics* (January, 1991), an article entitled "Getting Kids to Bed: How Tough is Too Tough?" explored pediatric viewpoints on many of the problems we have discussed in this chapter. Interestingly, the sample of pediatricians interviewed indicated a predictable split: some were in general agreement with the kind of policies I am describing; others were opposed on the grounds that "deeper" causes than merely manipulative behavior, such as separation anxiety and regression, were at stake.

One pediatrician, convinced that sleep problems originate in legitimate fears of the bedroom or nighttime in general, suggested that the child be allowed to sleep on the floor in the parents' bedroom, or to choose any location in the house except the parents' bed. Another stated categorically: "If you look just a little beyond the refusenik's immediate behavior, it is obvious that most of these children *need* to be out of the bedroom at all costs or are fearful of separation."

Needless to say, I disagree. Letting your child occupy the floor of your bedroom achieves the same net outcome as letting him sleep in your bed: In effect, the child controls the bedroom. You certainly are not free to initiate unplanned lovemaking in the middle of the night with your two-year-old sleeping on the carpet a few feet away. Nor do you have any feeling of privacy left whatsoever. That is bound to take its toll.

Assuming that "refusenik" marauders "*need* to be out of the bedroom at all costs or are fearful of separation" is to assume that manipulative behavior is not a normal part of childhood. I think it is. So does Barton D.

Schmitt, director of consultation services at Children's Hospital in Denver. Dr. Schmitt also recommends enforcing bedtime boundaries by locking the door—a recommendation which brings bristled responses from the other sector of pediatricians who label Schmitt's approach a "reign of terror." Schmitt's supporters, such as Dr. Glenn Austin of California, endorse the technique, noting that allowing the child to wander out of her room repeatedly and wake the parents

> ...creates anxiety and makes bedtime battles worse. Parents who keep losing sleep become angry, and even permissive parents often end up scolding, shaking the child, or spanking in anger. All of those punishments are worse than enforced isolation. It is better to lock the child in and get it over with. After about three nights, most children...decide that the parents mean business.... Then these children calm down because, finally, the rules are clear and consistent and the parents aren't frustrated with or angry at them any more."

Dr. Austin continues his positive evaluation:

> For 35 years in primary pediatric practice, I have advised locking the child in his bedroom if he refuses to stay there when told. Because I follow most of my patients through college, and often beyond, I feel comfortable that this practice does no psychological damage.

I might just as well have written the above quotation. However, ultimately the issue of how you, as parents, handle your child's sleep problems will not be decided by a group of debating, disagreeing pediatricians. You can certainly use our opinions as a springboard to elicit your own values and sentiments on the topic, but by no means it is wise to simply adopt one approach or another simply because it is endorsed or panned by an "expert." Read the differing methods and their rationales and see what fits for you.

Do you sense a deeper problem brewing beneath your child's recalcitrant nighttime behavior? Or does it feel like the push of a growing child trying to test certain boundaries? The answer to these two questions will automatically point you in one direction or another: toward professional help for additional diagnosis and treatment, or toward self-designed, pragmatic solutions to normal developmental trials.

If you neglect to set verbal and physical limits, your charming nine-month-old sleep monster will grow into a not-so-adorable fifteen-year-old, whose seemingly benign but manipulative ways have grown and multiplied through years of daily practice. When you do what feels right to you, then in all likelihood, it will be right for your baby. You have a right to enjoy your life, to *not be* consumed by your children, to be your own person. This does not mean that you're taking anything away from your children. On the contrary, you're really giving them *more*.]

R

Prescription for Winning at Sleeping

1. Examine your expectations about when your baby should and should not sleep. Remind yourself that sleep is a product of two factors: your baby's unique needs, coupled with the fact that *sleep is a habit* that your baby learns. Put the two together and you get:

   Sleep is a unique pattern that your baby learns to do on a habitual basis.

2. *Never bargain for bedtime.* Set limitations for sleep time based on your child's unique needs, and then let the toddler sleep or not sleep, as he or she chooses.

3. Learn to distinguish between types of crying, and then *trust your perceptions.*

4. Remember that *crying is as normal as testing.* It is a form of pre-verbal communication and does not necessarily signal distress.

5. If your baby stops her nighttime crying the moment you pick her up, you can be fairly certain that her crying is attention-related rather than pain-related. *Put her back down, leave her night-light on, and leave the room.*

6. Having determined that your baby is safe, comfortable, and healthy, *let her cry.*

7. Resist the urge to let your toddler sleep with you at night. Even after a nightmare, *keep him in his own room.*

8. If your toddler has turned into a "midnight marauder," consider using physical restrictions for a period of time. Remember that *real communication is the art of demonstrating your position on a given issue, whether via words or actions.*

9. As your child gets older, allow him the bedtime of his choice, *but don't let his choice influence the time he has to get up in the morning.*

10. Do not require napping unless your child demonstrates a need for it.

6 ❧

Eat, Eat, Eat— And Be Wary

Food can be used as an agent of control by either the parent or the child. The child who barely touches his supper but then awakens his parents in the middle of the night to tell them he is starving is using food as an agent of control. So, too, can the parent misuse the power of food to bribe, cajole, and otherwise lure a child into an unwanted activity.

Feeding is often equated with loving. When baby cries and we quiet him through feeding, we feel we are giving love. The more mashed bananas we can coax into his mouth, the more love we are giving—so we think—until that infant grows into an adult who can't even be seen in swimming trunks because of all that love he got as a kid.

Love is the opposite of over-feeding. It is the direct antithesis of coercing an already full infant into one more bite by doing a Fred Astaire two-step in front of the high chair. *To love your infant is to allow him to tell you when he is full.* Today's overfed and over-loved adults who search for culinary surcease in such organizations as Overeater's Anonymous, The Schick Center, Weight Watchers and the like, undoubtedly were infants whose parents would not let them turn down the last bite.

Eating. Forty percent of us do it mostly when no one's looking, for all the wrong reasons, and in all the wrong places—behind supply cabinets, in public washrooms, even while driving when the only person who can see the gallon of rocky road between our legs is the bus driver. (Over 10 percent of us keep forks and spoons in the glove compartment). Some of us eat standing up because we feel too guilty to sit down and the ones who sit down are often too full to stand up.

When it comes to food, parents are presented with countless opportunities to step into either side of the consuming/consumed cycle. In Philip Roth's book, *Portnoy's Complaint*, Portnoy's mother typifies the consuming mother who dedicates her life to the pursuit of feeding her family. Our obsession with eating knows no ethnic or categorical boundaries—it is clearly every parent's syndrome. I call it an obsession because we are a nation obsessed with food. We spend one sixth of our lives eating, another precious eighth thinking about eating, and who knows how much time feeling guilty for having eaten.

The activity of eating has become much more than the process of refueling our bodies; Americans have made it a moral issue full of rewards, punishment, and hang-ups. The first seeds of misunderstanding and anxiety are planted when the infant is barely adjusted to the new environment and the new environment has barely adjusted to the infant. We hardly know this infant before we are lamenting, "She's not eating enough," "She hardly eats at all," "She hasn't eaten in a week."

Although loss of appetite or no appetite may signal illness during the first four to six years, the baby who "has not eaten all week" is usually the progeny of confused, scared, new parents who equate a baby who eats with gusto with a good job of parenting. They are too nervous, however, to really notice what the infant eats—only what she *doesn't* eat. Thus, the baby of the parents who have told me "She hasn't eaten all week," is usually the one who shows a one pound weight gain in 12 days.

One parent, who insisted that her four-month-old baby never ate, couldn't understand how he had gained over two pounds in one month. While no one admits to feeding him on the sly, it is hard to imagine the four-month-old running off to the refrigerator for snacks.

The flip side of this coin occurs when a parent asks, "How do you stop a child from eating candy and cookies all day long?" I have difficulty with the image that comes to mind of a three-year-old running off to the market for candy and cookies. In 1968 Americans broke a record in the per capita consumption of candy bars and cookies. According to the Department of Commerce, each man, woman, and child consumed an average of 25.1 pounds a year of confectionery food items. By 1975, the average was down to 16.7 pounds, and by 1985, it was up to 19.1. The Federal Agency clearly stated that adults are the largest consumers. My message to parents of pre-schoolers, therefore, is simple: IF IT DOESN'T GET INTO THE HOUSE, IT WON'T GET INTO THE STOMACH.

The Menu:
Consumed or Consuming?

*One of the most fascinating and truly
astounding aspects of modern American
culture is the tremendous impact upon
parent-child relationships that the
simple act of eating so often produces.
In this respect, it is perhaps rivaled
only by the inane over-attention that
is similarly paid to toilet training.*

—William Homan

Because food is such a powerful, primary reinforcer, it can easily become the vehicle through which the consuming/consumed cycle of parenting is rooted into the family's life. Parents begin their journey into parenthood with no apprenticeship to fall back on. Suddenly, they are confronted with screams, cries and wails that signal, in their minds and hearts, the very worst. To stop the crying the mother picks up her disgruntled infant and either gives him her nipple or a bottle...and he stops crying...She puts him down again and the baby screams...She picks him up again and feeds him more. Sooner or later, the baby either figures out how to manipulate the mother, or the mother gets locked into manipulating the baby's mood (making him "happy") by feeding him. Either way, you've got the beginnings of consumed and consuming parenting. The consumed parent will end up dodging the food being thrown at her by her toddler, who has learned to wield this powerful weapon; and the consuming parent will end up overfeeding and over-controlling the child's diet. The consumed parent is a caterer, running a 24-hour cafeteria in an attempt to keep the child happy; the consuming parent is a strict dietician whose cafeteria closes on time.

In distinguishing between consumed and consuming behavior in relation to food, the question becomes: *Who's got control?* For the consumed parent, the child has control: "I won't eat this...I want that...I don't want that..." and the parent accommodates. When the parent is consuming, the child is in a more passive position as the parent dictates which foods should be consumed. Often, parents experience a complete turnabout in their parenting style around the issue of food. They begin in the consuming mode, doting over their baby, overfeeding their baby. Then, the moment comes when the baby or toddler realizes that food can be used to manipulate. Depending on the personality and disposition of the parent, a major shift can take place whereby the parent who was on the offensive—trying to control everything the baby ate—now moves to a defensive position of bargaining, pleading, and cajoling.

I have noticed that overweight parents who were overly restricted with regard to food as children have a particularly difficult time setting guidelines or appropriate restrictions for their own children. It comes as no surprise to me that these parents equate any kind of food restriction with deprivation. Bringing the issue out into the open—seeing how their early experiences are now affecting how they are parenting—seems to help overweight parents change their patterns of indulgence with their children.

If I were three years old (and I once was), I would say to myself, "Why eat what's good for me? Why eat what will make me grow big? Why eat peas because kids are starving in Africa?" What's more, if I were between two and six years old and knew my mother and father got upset when I refused breakfast and knew they couldn't stand letting me wait until lunch, I'd realize that my chances for raisins, cookies, and snacks between meals were excellent. In fact, I'd soon realize that they were thrilled to see me eat. My bargaining power with them would certainly be increased as I endeavored to "thrill" them more often. Also, if I were still a youngster and realized that when I behaved obnoxiously, people quieted me with cookies, I'd strive to be more obnoxious!

If we assume we have a healthy, thriving infant/child and there is a feeding problem, we must realize that, as parents, we have either created it or nurtured it. Most of it is *our* problem, not the child's. I don't say this to be accusatory, only to help us all relax around the realization that the children are usually fine, with one exception—they have parents with "food hang-ups." All adults have food preferences—likes and dislikes, foods that they eat as often as possible, and foods that they refuse to eat. Yet a parent who herself refuses to eat squash will insist that her toddler eat it "because it's good for him." It is important to understand that a child's culinary preferences can be trusted and should be respected.

Of all the problems that have roots reaching back to the beginning of your relationship with your infant, and that carry over to affect other behavior problems as the infant grows, the eating problem may be the most significant. No problem preoccupies the American public more than the eating habits of its children. In 29 years of general pediatric practice I have never heard a parent or grandparent say, "My, isn't the baby's weight *just right!*" Our infants are either too thin or too fat, or *seem* to be getting too thin or too fat. Our perceptions in this area are clouded with old guilt and hand-me-down confusion—passed on like family birthmarks, from one generation to the next.

Recently I encountered my first startlingly positive experience with a parent on this issue of food consumption. After doing a routine physical exam on her 3½-year-old son, which he passed with "flying colors,"

I asked the mother if she were having problems with Elliott's mealtimes like she had had with Sarah, her five-year-old daughter.

"No," she answered. "I decided that he's responsible for what he chooses to eat or not eat."

That, I thought, was a marvelous statement. I also realized that it takes a certain amount of courage to enforce. We are so obsessed with making sure the baby gets a "well-balanced meal" that we forget that the baby may also know a thing or two. A baby who is repeatedly pushing the food away or spitting it out is communicating a message and making a choice. In our over-zealousness as parents, we forget that babies are born with a natural ability to communicate what they want or don't want. Parents who become too concerned (consuming) about their child's food consumption can pose just as much of a problem as parents who are indulgent (consumed). When the parent becomes fanatical about making sure the child drinks all the milk, or making sure that equal amounts of the major food groups have been eaten, then you've got the beginnings of another form of food hang-up.

Early Fat Deposits

Our bodies are able to function quite frugally on the metabolic motto, "Waste not, want not." We use up what we need to meet our energy expenditures and very efficiently store away the rest. Yet, we stuff our infants as if they were hibernating animals who must endure long periods of caloric deprivation—forgetting that they, too, store excess food as adipose tissue—or, in plain language—FAT! Perhaps we don't realize that in human beings, caloric deprivation rarely exceeds the time-span between meals.

In our country the root cause of obesity in 25 to 45

percent of the people who are overweight can be found in eating patterns established in early infancy. When we force-feed or worry-feed a child, *we are helping that child to form three times as many fat cells than he will need to maintain a normal weight throughout life.* There is no way to make fat cells go away when weight becomes a real problem later. Obese adults can never reduce the number of actual fat cells in their bodies; they can only reduce the amount of total fat content within each fat cell. In essence, they must learn to keep their "cellular sponges" wrung out, lest apple pie and pizza find three times as much space in which to become body fat.

Most of the eating problems of children in this country are sandwiched between two primary parental penchants. First, *this is the land of plenty, where providing food is a sign of caring and loving.* Second, *nothing must be wasted, because the old country wasn't so plentiful.* Therefore, we have a situation wherein we allow children to graze like cows all day long while insisting they eat like horses at mealtime.

Eating should give pleasure, but too much pleasure is not good either. Aside from the multiplication of fat cells which begins in early infancy, studies now show that certain hereditary forms of high cholesterol can be identified early in life—so not only will these infants have more fat cells, but more grist for the artery mill as well.

Breastfeeding

*For the following discussion on breastfeeding, I invited Lisa Garfield, M.P.H.,R.D., our resident nutritionist, to present her points of view, which sometimes differ from my preferences and opinions. There is never **only** one answer; but often there is one answer that is right for you.*

Long before solid foods were created, there was breast milk. Breastfeeding can be one of the most emotionally satisfying experiences for a new mother. Long before there were pediatricians to comment on it, or a La Leche League to recommend it, breastfeeding was being done by all mammals suckling their young. We human mammals, however, have managed to surround it in controversy by being either in favor of it or against it. Three decades ago, bottle-feeding was often preferred over breastfeeding; two decades ago, breastfeeding was heralded as the pinnacle experience of mother-child bonding—and so has reigned ever since. Organizations of all kinds have come out with what amounts to "policy statements" on the virtues and benefits of breastfeeding. Our national consciousness of it has risen sharply, so that pregnant mothers are frequently asked by friends and/or relatives, "Are you going to breastfeed?" A new mother taking her three-month old for a stroll in the park can be asked by a total stranger, "Are you breast-feeding?" It sometimes seems as if *everyone* has the right to know whether a mother is willing or unwilling to give her baby the benefit of her breasts.

If a mother *wants* to breastfeed, is comfortable doing it in her life situation, and is successful at it (produces enough milk), then I think it's wonderful for both mother and baby. However, I strenuously object to the atmosphere of *judgment* that currently surrounds the issue. *No one* has the right to tell a woman that she "should" breastfeed, or to imply or contend that she is doing something grossly wrong if she does not. Mothers who, for one reason or another, choose not to breastfeed are made to feel (1) that they are not "complete" as mothers, (2) that their babies won't thrive, and (3) that their babies' later development will suffer from the deprivation of breastfeeding.

As far as I know, there are no long-term studies that show that breastfed babies grow up to be healthier adults than bottle-fed babies. We do know that breastfed babies get a great deal of benefit from the mother's milk, because it's very healthy. *However*, we also now know that when a nursing mother is tense and anxious, the level of stress hormones circulating throughout her system rises sharply. What this means is that a mother who is uncomfortable nursing but does so out of guilt is not necessarily doing her baby any favors.

> *Lisa*: Breast milk is the ideal food for babies. It provides the correct proportion of protein, carbohydrates, and fats. It also provides immunological advantages in the first few months of life. There are rarely (if any) allergies. Recent longterm studies have emphasized that the immunological benefits of breast milk are short-term in that there is little difference *over time* in the incidence of colds between breastfed and bottle-fed babies. Thus, while breast milk provides an immunological "edge" in the first few months, this *does not* mean that breastfed babies become healthier children than bottle-fed babies.

> *Dr. Zukow*: Breast milk is ideal only if the process of breastfeeding is working—if the mother enjoys it, is not exhausted physically, and the baby is gaining. If any of these criteria are not present, it is advisable to switch to bottle-feeding. Even though bottle-feeding is not *equal* to breastfeeding, it is *as good*. In my perspective, what is of primary importance is the *experience of feeding*, not so much whether it is delivered through a bottle or a breast.

Lisa: In third-world countries where sanitation and economics are a problem, breastfeeding should be encouraged. It is more sanitary than bottles that cannot be boiled due to lack of heat and running water. It is also more economical, and third-world mothers cannot dilute it (like they can formula) to last longer, thereby decreasing the nutritional value to their children.

In this country it is usually a question of the mother's lifestyle, not sanitation. Also, most children do (or should) receive immunizations to protect against major illness. But in the first months before immunizations can be given, breastfeeding gives an immunological edge.

It takes a lot of work to breastfeed. A mother has to remember to rest, to drink fluids (8 cups or more), and to increase her caloric intake by 500 calories per day. She may have to accept a slower weight loss (or none at all) to keep her calories and milk production up. When the baby goes through a growth spurt, she may be feeding every two hours, sometimes one hour apart. That means she just finishes feeding when she has to start again. It may take 20 to 40 minutes to nurse some babies. But, she has the advantage of convenience. She doesn't have to spend time boiling bottles and nipples; she doesn't have to carry bottles, then warm them while she is out. And she may enjoy the emotional satisfaction caused not only by the bonding but by the release of natural endorphins that are relaxing and mood-enhancing.

Let me hasten to add, however, that breastfeeding *per se* does not promote bonding. If the breastfeeding mother is exhausted and stressed by the activity, an atmstpshere of bonding will not prevail. It should also be stated clearly that *bottle-fed babies bond just as well as breastfed babies.*

Dr. Zukow: I would like to emphasize that in addition to the physical energy required for breastfeeding, the mother needs to realize that it also takes a lot of mental/emotional energy. Breastfeeding is not just a physical experience. It has two equally important components: the physical and physiological is one part, and the mother's internal state-of-being is the other part. Often, mothers have a difficult time breastfeeding their first baby because they are anxious about whether or not they will be able to produce enough milk, and they are anxious in general in their new role as mother. This anxiety, as I have mentioned, affects the mother's physiology, which includes her breast milk. Once this stage of anxiety is overcome (*if* it is overcome), the mental/emotional component of breastfeeding evens out and no longer presents an added problem. Usually, breastfeeding the second baby is a far more successful experience for the mother than the first experience.

Regarding the next point—that the mother may need to breastfeed every two hours during growth spurts—Lisa and I are in complete (but friendly) disagreement. I do not think a mother ever needs to breastfeed every two hours. Babies are in a continuous process of growth, so I'm not sure the concept of a "growth spurt" is really valid, physiologically or nutritionally speaking. I suspect it is more an emotional need. If the breast milk is rich enough, a three-to-four-week-old baby should not need to be fed more often than every four hours. If the baby cries for more,

I would suspect it is the *experience of feeding* the baby is asking for: the closeness, the warmth, the voice, the touch. The mother can give as much of that as she wants, without requiring herself to breastfeed every two hours, with a scant 30 minutes of free time in-between.

Lisa: The bottle-feeding mother may have more freedom away from the baby. She can sleep and get needed rest while father or another caretaker feeds the baby. She will still have to feed the baby on the chosen schedule, but she has the flexibility of feeding in all public places without the possibility of "offending" others. (Yes, some people are still offended by breastfeeding.)

So the question of whether to breastfeed or bottle-feed is truly a personal choice—a question of lifestyle and comfort levels. Once a mother does decide to breastfeed, I highly recommend that she take a class on breastfeeding, which teaches the basic principles and techniques that foster self-confidence in the mother. In general, breastfeeding classes suggest that new mothers establish their milk supply and make sure the baby has adjusted well to breastfeeding before introducing a supplemental or replacement bottle. There are several reasons for this recommendation. One is that supplementing too early may decrease the mother's milk production. The more a mother nurses, the more milk she produces. Another reason stems from the fact that sucking from the breast uses different mouth muscles than sucking from a bottle. Since it may be easier for some babies to suck from the bottle, a baby during the first six to eight weeks may begin to prefer the bottle. Rejecting the mother's breast for a bottle is upsetting for the mother and usually triggers a decrease in her milk supply. However, once the mother's supply and routine are established, supplementation may be introduced without disruption.

Dr. Zukow: Regarding supplementing breastfeeding with bottle feedings, my feeling is, if breastfeeding every four hours is working, there is no need to add supplements. If it is not, than supplements are indicated. However, I disagree that using supplements automatically decreases the mother's milk supply. If a baby is still hungry after breastfeeding, the baby will happily take a supplement, which in turn relaxes the mother and *increases* her milk supply. Also remember that the quality of mother's milk will vary throughout the day, so there naturally will be times when the baby isn't fully satiated by the breast. This is normal and not indicative of failure on the mother's part.

As for taking classes on breastfeeding, I think that's fine as long as the instructors do not make mothers feel guilty if they stop breastfeeding. I feel it is destructive for lactation consultants to express, verbally or nonverbally, a belief in the superiority of breastfeeding over bottle-feeding. Such a perspective only causes distress in mothers who are already experiencing conflict over breastfeeding.

As a pediatrician I have seen many overwrought mothers—some feeling anxious about breastfeeding but doing it anyway, and others not doing it but feeling racked with guilt over "not being a good mother." I tell mothers that the important point is that *feeding take place in an environment of comfort and lovingness.* It is that environment that will ensure the thriving development of the baby, not whether or not breastfeeding occurs. How does the breast-less father bond? How does the mother who cannot nurse bond? Bonding is not a function of a nipple in the mouth with milk coming out of it; it is a function of the way the parent and the baby connect emotionally, physically, through all kinds of verbal and touch communication. You can have an abusive mother who breastfeeds.

Breastfeeding can become the starting point of consumed/consuming parenting: Every time the baby cries, the mother nurses. This supposedly promotes bonding to the utmost. What it also promotes, unfortunately, is a kind of *addiction to bonding* whereby the mother only feels good about her mothering when she is satisfying her baby's needs. There are mothers who breastfeed their babies hourly, believing that this creates a secure and happy baby. What it is more likely to create is a baby who knows exactly how to manipulate you. The consuming mother might be compulsively breastfeeding from the vantage point of "This constitutes love and bonding," while the consumed mother is trying to squelch her fears of the baby's crying and her sense of inadequacy at the sound of discomfort. Breastfeeding fulfills two set of needs: the mother's and the baby's. The problem is, the baby doesn't always need it.

Eating:
The "Parent-Pleasing" Coin

Poor eating habits concern me not only from the standpoint of physical health; in addition, they easily become weapons in a warehouse of behavior problems. How and what the child eats becomes a well-honed, manipulative tool, so that sitting down to eat becomes a debacle of emotional surgery.

CONSUMED MOTHER to child: "Eat your peas."

Child: "I don't want to!" [to prove his point the toddler throws himself on the ground and flails his arms and legs in protest].

CONSUMED MOTHER to child: "If you eat your peas, you can have ice cream."

The child of the consuming parent already knows that if she eats the peas, she'll get the ice cream because she'll make her mother happy. The consuming parent exerts tremendous effort to control what enters her child's mouth. How does the consuming parent get the child to eat what she wants? By giving the child no choices and by rewarding eating behavior. The child is motivated to please the consuming parent because pleasing, in turn, nets rewards.

The consumed parent never gets a chance to reward; she is always treading water, fielding refusals, pleading. The child of the consumed parent gets what he wants directly by acting out, as we saw in our above example.

Feeding the infant is so easy now that from the beginning it should not require too much effort. The belief that all babies eat the same amount of food and milk is untrue. To assume that everyone's cellular metabolism is the same is like saying we all wear the same size shoe. There are many eating fallacies. One might be infant night-feeding. I'm still not sure there is good evidence to support a night-feeding in the hospital. I have had many newborns as young as 10 days give up middle-of-the-night feedings.

Eating is a habit, and habits range from one extreme to the other. Have you ever noticed how infants and small children tend to repeat things that make parents smile?

Children intuitively strive to improve their self-image by pleasing us. Unfortunately, from infancy they have picked up on every nuance of our expression as we try to spoon-feed one last bit of cottage cheese into an unwilling mouth. They learn early (from us) that we put all our "self-image eggs" in one basket, and that basket is called mealtime. We need to realize that *when we treat mealtime any other way but routinely, we are giving the infant a powerful weapon.*

An example of the child's desire to please is demonstrated by the toddler who, after being a poor eater, suddenly begins to eat everything in sight with such progressive voraciousness that by the time she is three or four, a padlock for the refrigerator is indicated. Parents think that perhaps she's having a growing spurt or suffering from tapeworm. Very few recognize that the child is simply trying to please parents whose eyes light up at the sight of food going into her mouth. On the other side of this parent-pleasing coin is the scenario of the child now angry at authority (specifically, at parents) who uses withdrawal from all nourishing food as her ultimate weapon.

Food is food, to be eaten when our bodies need it. Yet, parents make productions out of infant feedings that would rival Ziegfeld in extravagances. We fly the spoons like airplanes into baby's mouth, tap our fingers on the high chair like a rhythm band—all in all, producing, directing, and choreographing an entire show just so baby will take five instead of four spoonsful of applesauce. One attitude should prevail at mealtime:

Follow a consistent routine of allowing baby to empty her stomach between meals; at mealtime, offer her reasonable choices of nutritious foods, allow her to make judgments on taste and quantity, and then clear the food away without prejudicial comment.

Almost every parent is confronted with the supreme challenge of getting food down an infant who is more interested in spitting it back. Even though the baby is hungry, he or she prefers to feel the food dribble back out the mouth and down the chin. Some spitting back is normal, especially when the baby is experimenting with different textures and colors. But what do you do about it? Do you sit there for 45 minutes going through the above repertory? I think it's far more efficient for you and beneficial for the baby to take the baby "at his word." The challenge is to learn to distinguish when the baby is spitting back the food as a way of saying, "No more," and when he is experimenting with it. Once you've determined it's the former case, that can be the end of it. Or sort of. Once the baby is crawling, the moment you put him down from the high chair he is off in the direction of the refrigerator. The next thing you know, he is knocking on the refrigerator door and crying. It is hard for parents to learn to say, "Too bad, mealtime is over." But babies and toddlers need to learn that there is a beginning and an end to mealtime. Otherwise you wind up trying to feed your baby all day long.

Introducing New Foods

When introducing new foods to infants or toddlers, you stand a better chance of succeeding if it can be done in a calm environment. If there are a lot of distracting things going on such as TV, siblings fighting, and door bells ringing, then chances are high that the child won't want to take the opportunity to experiment because he's so preoccupied. Ideally, you arrange a time when the older kids are outside and you can control the environment, and you quietly introduce the new food to your baby. *Realistically*, what is more likely to occur is, just as you are showing your child chicken pieces for the first time, your phone rings and your husband tells you the mortgage check has just bounced; the doorbell rings with a courier package you have to sign for; and three kids of indeterminate origin come sweeping through the house in search of snacks. Not only does the baby throw up from all the commotion, but you throw up as well! As I said, *ideally* you can *try* to introduce new foods in a quiet environment.

If the child becomes obsessed with one particular food, the parent can safely allow that one food to be consumed while continuing to introduce other foods at intervals, always letting choice remain with the child. Eventually the child will move on to select a different food item because he will get bored with his current food obsession.

I can cite a very recent example. One of my patients is a wiry four-year-old who is chronically constipated. She is thin as a rail, just like her mother. We talked about the constipation and about eating patterns. The mother told me she herself was a "lousy eater." I wondered to myself, what are the chances of the child being a good eater if the mother is a lousy eater? The mother told me that the only thing her daughter would eat were peanut butter and baloney sandwiches. Their mealtimes had become war zones of constant fighting.

In desperation, the mother said that she would do anything.

As soon as she said that I said, "Okay. Let your daughter eat the peanut butter on toast three or four times a day, and if she wants to throw in a baloney sandwich, fine. You know that at some point in her life, she's going to develop some specific tastes and those tastes are not always going to be for peanut butter or baloney."

Four days later the mother called me: "You're not going to believe this, but we haven't had a single fight at mealtime. She just stuffs that damn peanut butter down her mouth. She can't wait to take it to lunch. And she's not constipated!"

I have all the faith in the world that this mother's child will eventually expand her food preferences. It is important to keep a sane perspective when confronted by obstinate and obsessional eating patterns in children. The insane perspective has parents living in full dread that nothing but peanut butter will *ever* pass their child's lips. The sane perspective has parents remembering that children develop different tastes at different points along the way. Patience and equanimity will win out, if given the chance.

All Solid Foods Are Not Created Equal

In the field of pediatrics, views on nutrition have undergone tremendous change. In regard to guidelines in infant feeding, we've gone from advocating *on demand*, to *semi-demand*, to combinations of the two and back. Currently there is even more flux regarding the optimal time to introduce solid foods. In the recent past, the American Academy of Pediatrics decreed that solid foods started too early led to allergies, cholesterol problems, and obesity. The Academy even held pediatricians responsible for having created a generation of obese people, claiming that if infants were kept on formula longer, instead of being switched to low-fat or whole milk, the problem would have been avoided. (My view is that it is fine to switch to milk as long as the baby's weight and iron levels remain optimal and precluding any cow's milk allergies.)

I do not think that starting a baby on solid foods too early *per se* causes immediate or later weight problems;

nor does the switch from formula to milk *per se*. The real culprit in childhood weight problems stems from one of two sources, both of which lay in the laps of the parents: either the parents themselves have poor (high fat) eating habits, which they pass on to the child; or the parents over-emphasize food as a reinforcer. We all know that food is a powerful reinforcer, probably rivaled only by the parent's smile in its impact on behavior. It is all too easy to use food, sweets especially, to quiet the baby, to distract the toddler, to keep the four-year-old sitting in the basket in the supermarket. Thin parents can just as easily raise a child with an eating problem as parents who are overweight or even obese. However, it should also be noted that research has indicated that a strong genetic predisposition to overweight can also be the source of the problem. Whatever the source or sources of the weight problem, to treat only the child would be like Windexing the mirror every time you didn't like what you saw in it.

Fortunately, most of the salt and sugar has been removed from commercial baby foods within the last few years. Osterizers and blenders can provide excellent nutrition and guilt-free food attitudes for parents. The parents I know who are willing to grind up their own baby food are very content and self-satisfied that the foods they are providing contain no unnecessary fillers, food additives, artificial flavors, or colorings.

Of course, the baby must be developmentally ready for solid foods. If you put a spoon in a child's mouth and he keeps spitting it out, obviously he is either not interested or not ready. There are some babies who, no matter what you put in their mouths, they are going to swallow. And there are other babies who really don't know how to swallow the solid food yet. If you have doubt about the readiness of your baby to accept solid food, talk to your pediatrician.

My policy is, begin introducing solid foods by the time an infant is eight weeks old if she is taking 32 ounces of milk a day and is still hungry. If the child is chubby by the time she is 2½ years old, then it's because she's shopping with Mom at the deli—not because creamed corn was introduced to her in her infancy. Let me quickly add that I am totally against putting solid food in bottles so that a baby can feed herself without the mother taking time to spoon feed the food. The child winds up with a bottle that is four ounces of formula, one-half jar of vegetables, and one-half jar of cereal. While that combination of food is not unhealthy, the method of providing it goes a long a way toward establishing a very bad habit. At six to seven months of age that mother is going to have one awful time trying to get her baby to learn to feed herself with spoons and forks. Babies love to suck and giving them a bottle of "suckable" solid food is like giving them an oral intravenous; they will suck on it all day long.

Weight Problems Start With the *What*, Not the *When*

Cookies, snack chips, biscuits, sugar-loaded cereals—these are all solid but poor foods. Since baby food is not exactly a gourmet taste treat, it is a rare infant who will refuse the sugary, crunchy, and frosting-rich offerings. But introducing the cookie or snack (especially between meals) is what starts the bad habit; introducing food to the child (particularly the 2- to 2½-year-old) to alleviate boredom is a bad habit; and introducing dessert at the end of each meal is a bad habit. Weight problems come from an early reliance on the wrong solid foods for the wrong reason, not on solid foods in and of themselves.

Television is probably your worst enemy in trying to instill sane eating habits in your child. Sweets and fatty foods parade across TV screens from the first morning cartoons to the last evening program viewed by the child. I certainly have no magic solution to this ever-present source of propaganda, other than to remain firm and consistent in *not* stocking these foods.

You can't put a chubby five-year-old on a thousand-calorie-a-day-diet. Most adults can't even cope with that degree of regimentation and deprivation. What you can do is very discreetly begin diminishing the quantity of food that is offered, a teaspoon at a time. That way it's almost unnoticeable. If the child is used to having a whole baked potato, for example, give him only three-quarters of one. If he's used to having two lamb chops, give him one and a half. Slowly but surely, decrease the caloric intake so that his requirements get less and less—almost painlessly. Using this method is one way of avoiding the "deprivation mentality" whereby the mother is continually in the position of telling the kid, "You can't have this, you can't have that." Instead she is slowly nudging her child toward a healthy weight loss without becoming the "bad guy."

Many of us want to look like Jane Fonda, or the new Dolly Parton, or Arnold Schwartzenegger, or Sylvester Stallone, or any other perfect physical specimen. We can become so self-conscious that we suddenly want our children, who don't understand, to give up food which tastes good and start running nine miles a day! It won't work. You have to be incredibly motivated to lose weight. But besides being motivated, I think there is something important about wanting to be who you are, and enjoying who you are, and having a self-image that is good. If we say that a child who is five or ten pounds overweight is fat, we're not helping his self-image. If this is a child who is getting along fine in school and has a friendly relationship with his peers, why make a big fuss about five or ten pounds? Eventually he's going to find things that are more interesting and compelling to do than eat. In the meantime, you can consult your pediatrician and/or nutritionist for some low-key dietary guidelines. The important point is to *avoid creating an overweight or fat identity* in your child.

The Hungry Twos

The twos are terrible in part because of the problems parents create during the first 12-18 months. By age two, the child is becoming adept at manipulative behavior; she knows how to cry when food is refused, because she has previously learned how important her eating is to the parents. After all, from 12-18 months most of the day is spent trying to get her to eat by cajoling, dancing, airplane-spoon-into-mouth trick, and on and on. Understand that allowing her to cry for long periods of time will cause her no harm or hernias, and consigning her to her room will not demonstrate rejection—only that you will not tolerate a food whiner.

This is the stage when parents have the choice either to set firm limits at the refrigerator and cookie jar, or to end up being cafeteria managers for the next several years. (Desserts are totally unnecessary in an infant's or small child's diet and only set patterns for later cravings. I believe very strongly that introducing desserts with meals must have come from the fact that the food was so terrible, something sweet was needed to cover up the bad taste!) Remember that by giving in to the toddlers' food whims, you are denying her the experience of developing proper eating habits.

Age Two-and-One-Half On

By this age, eating habits are fairly well set. Remember that part of the problem is that children now belong to the "run and eat" crowd. Their activity and ability to move (and they are probably in constant motion) has increased tremendously. Setting a time to eat is to your advantage. This may keep you out of the "cafeteria-short-order-cook" syndrome.

The growth of school-age children has already been determined by past eating habits, and they now need food for energy. (I'm not referring to poverty areas where true malnutrition affects linear growth and delays development.) School-aged children do not do marketing, so what they are exposed to depends on your judgment. From the very young to the teenager, children become super conscious of food, mainly from their exposure to various advertising promotions, especially on television, which give them misinformation and false expectations. Kids see some tiger with cereal and they want that cereal. When they go to the market they start screaming for it, so the mother gets it for them—or refuses and buys a low-sugar cereal, which the kids refuse to eat because they want the tiger! The cereal battle can be solved easily enough by having the tiger one week and the low-fat, low-sugar cereal the next. Compromise! But the larger problem is one of media influence. How can parents solve the problem of the media's influence over their children's eating habits? With effort, to say the least. Parents just have to take a stand on what their eating policy is and then enforce it. But lest you rest too soon on your laurels of accomplishment, don't forget the kid next door who gets to eat Hershey bars and drink cokes. "George next door gets to, so why can't I?" then becomes the whining litany of the week. Obviously you can't go into a long explanation with a four-year-old about the nutritional content of various foods. Nor is the "body image" argument any good at that age. A simple statement of fact, "It's not good for you," plus your firm and consistent enforcement, is your only hope for maintaining control over your child's eating habits.

Here again, though, I hasten to add an addendum to my own statement. Being firm and consistent doesn't mean becoming utterly rigid and inflexible. An attitude of rigidity and absolutism can lead to its own dangerous opposite—a bingeing mentality which, in turn, can lead to the serious disorders of anorexia and/or bulimia.

A recent news program on Channel 4 entitled "Life in the Fat Lane" reported that there are 50% more overweight children today than there were five years ago. The overall message of the program was, the problem of overweight is growing rapidly in our population. The solution?—drastically reduce the fat content of foods we feed to our babies, and for adults (what we've all known all along) lower our intake of fats and sugars and participate in regular exercise—for the rest of our lives.

Another news tidbit reported in *TV Guide* contained the shocking information that it is not uncommon for teenagers with their own VCRs to watch nine to 10 hours of television a day. They tape programs while they are at school and then watch their sets from three in the afternoon until midnight! Studies have found a significant, linear relationship between the number of hours spent watching television (or sitting in front of a computer screen) and the incidence of obesity in children. We are definitely into a new era. In "my day," kids either had paper routes after school, or played vigorously in the park or on their neighborhood streets. Now there is a whole generation or more of parents who have never heard of "Kick the Can" or "Capture the Flag."

What does all this have to do with your child's eating habits? It is to say that you've got some pretty stiff competition in this age of television commercials, video screens, and VCRs. And it is to underscore the very real importance of exposing your baby from day one to eating habits that will support his growth and well-being for the rest of his life. All obese adults had parents responsible for feeding them during their most impressionable periods of time. The way they were fed turned out to be no small matter!

When parents are concerned about why their children are fat, they can fall back on the genetic explanation; they can fall back on the fat-cell theory explanation. But probably the biggest influence is the influence that their own parental habits have had on their children, together with what is flashing on the television screen. I have seen parents who themselves eat healthfully, and who have raised their children from infancy on low-fat, low-sugar diets, still be confronted by the battle over bad food as a result of peer and media influence. Clearly, there is no pat answer to this issue. Even your best combination of factors—healthy parental eating habits, healthy eating habits established from infancy—can leave you vulnerable to potent external factors with which you will have to contend.

The good news is that parents today are so much more educated about nutrition that it is a pleasure to counsel them. I give very straightforward advice: Throughout all of these stages, offer your children nutritious selections and then respect their likes and dislikes—keeping in mind that few of us would actually prefer meat loaf or peas to ice cream!

Pleasure Before Nutrition

Mealtime is not the time of togetherness it once was.

According to psychologist-sociologist Paul A. Fine, who has conducted over 100 food studies, our feelings about mealtimes do not mesh with the reality of mealtime in America today. From extensive research it has been found that although breakfast carries great symbolic significance by representing family togetherness and a robust good start, less than 25 percent of American households engage in the ritual. Dr. Fine depicts the usual morning scene in America as follows:

> A youngster eats a bowl of cereal alone at the kitchen table before leaving for school. Another young child munches a piece of raisin bread while walking to school. The wife breakfasts standing up, having only coffee, and the father grabs a Danish pastry and coffee during 10 A.M. break at his office.

Dr. Fine notes that as a result, we get so hungry before noon that we resort to munching or to ravaging our lunch bags, virtually becoming a snacking society. He cites the person responsible for family marketing as no more than an order-filler who holds to the fantasy of normal family eating habits, while the reality is that the family often snacks its way from one meal to the next.

In view of these statistics, try to plan at least one sit-down meal a day in your home. It will usually be dinner, and discussions around the dinner table should be family-oriented and informal. If daily togetherness is impossible, Sunday morning brunch is a good alternative. Because family get-togethers are becoming rare, here are suggestions for ensuring the pleasure of your family's mealtime company.

℞

Prescription for Winning at Eating

1. Give young children at play at least ten minutes to end their activities instead of ordering them in to dinner *immediately*.

2. Allow everyone to have as much or as little to eat as they desire.

3. Do not overload a toddler or young child's plate (you can always give seconds).

4. Do not make dessert time into an opportunity for bribery by telling children they can have the dessert only if they eat their dinner.

5. Do not use mealtime for personal attacks or scolding.

6. Make casual suggestions (do not insist) about trying new food.

7. Whoever cooks the meal (be it husband or wife) should sit down with the family and not just be the overseer who hovers nervously around, making sure every bite is consumed.

8. Get involved in the family conversations rather than in the family food consumption.

Food can be used as an agent of control by either the parent or the child. The child who barely touches his supper but then wakes his parents up in the middle of the night to tell them he is starving is using food as an agent of control. What parent can refuse a starving child who wants to eat at three o'clock in the morning? So, too, can the parent misuse the power of food to bribe, cajole, and otherwise lure a child into an unwanted activity. As I pointed out in the previous chapters, manipulative behavior of this kind is something we all fall into—children in the course of simply growing up, and parents in desperate efforts to maintain some semblance of control over those chaotic growing-up years. But, more often than not, we are all doing the best we can, and it is in that spirit that we can acknowledge our own uses and abuses of food in relation to both ourselves and our children.

Coping with eating problems, sleeping problems, behavior problems, and limit setting are all part of *becoming* a parent. They represent different stages of *our* maturation as well as that of our babies and children. We grow as they grow, as long as we remain willing to listen to two sometimes conflicting sets of needs: those of our children as well as *our own*.

7 ❧

Potty Training... Just Let It Be

The most important point to remember is that, unless a child is brain-damaged or has some organic impairment, he or she will become toilet trained—that's a guarantee. The less fuss and emotion surrounding the topic, the better.

This is the shortest chapter in the book because potty training is the easiest topic to discuss. Unfortunately, it is often the hardest experience for parents to go through. Many parents turn potty training into a giant, pressing concern when it could be a natural process actually initiated by the child. Potty training becomes a disaster when all other household issues become secondary to it. If you drop whatever you're doing in order to devote yourself to training your child on the toilet periodically throughout the day, then you're in need of new tactics.

Much of a pediatrician's practice is taken up with the bowel habits of his/her young patients, as viewed through the anxious eyes of the parents. Many parents worry needlessly about their child's lack of potty training, when the simple fact is that the child's anus is not sufficiently mature to be controlled. As in all aspects of child development, each child will mature at a unique pace. This is especially crucial to remember when in the presence of your neighbor or relative, whose 18-month-old has been using the potty for the past two months. Try not to compare; avoid, as much as possible, the "comparison mentality."

Over the past four decades parental attitudes toward potty training have relaxed considerably. Today's parents are far more willing to toilet train later than were parents of the 1940s. In most studies of current toilet training practices, about one in four children is trained prior to 24 months, over half accomplish it a few months past two years, and four in five are trained by age three. In other words, most children are potty trained between two and three years of age. Back in the 1940s one study showed that 60 percent of the children in the sample were potty trained by 18 months. However, current-day studies also report "new techniques" for toilet training children *before* 12 months of age, indicating an unfortunate resurgence of the "sooner is better" attitude.

No new technique can ensure that a child is physiologically ready to be toilet trained. Indeed, I don't think "techniques" are necessary at all. In my experience three basic ingredients determine the success of toilet training:

(1) The child must *understand* what the parent is trying to teach him or her to do;
(2) The child's anal and bladder sphincters must be mature enough to control the bowel movement;

(3) The child must have his or her own desire to be clean, dry, and not smell.

The moment you begin trying "new techniques" to accelerate the process, you are placing undo attention and emphasis on what should be allowed to happen naturally. Realize that the number of words written, spoken, argued, advised and pleaded on this subject are directed at the wrong individual. All children who are free of organic problems will become potty trained *in their own time*. If you think about it and look around at your adult friends, how many are *not* potty trained? None, I hope.

How do parents differ in their potty-training pit-falls? The consuming parent will introduce training too early and too vigorously. Charts, schedules, and special toilets will adorn the bathroom; gold stars will adhere to the potty report on the refrigerator; cookies will be doled out for bowel movements in the pot. This is often the point at which distressed mothers begin finding bowel movements hidden under couches or behind drapes. The child wants to please, but is not yet ready to use a toilet. Sometimes I think that, from the young child's perspective, the bowel movement is part of his body—part of *him*—and so there is an initial ambivalence about flushing it down the toilet. Hence, the safely hidden deposits!

One of my mothers, inclined toward the consuming end of the continuum, got off to a disconcerting start regarding her son's excrements. At the age of nine months she discovered a brilliantly yellow-colored stool, which sent her flying to my office in a panic, with the excrement encased in a see-through sandwich bag. Yellow Play-Doh, fortunately free of any toxic substances, turned out to be the offending culprit. She was so frightened by the experience, however, that she began to check her son's stools obsessively. I doubt that more than ten grams of excrement passed from one end of her son's alimentary canal to the other without her careful inspection. Once every two months or so, I was presented with a "questionable specimen."

When it came time to think about toilet training, the mother continued to overemphasize what should have been a natural process. She purchased a series of special potty seats (one was a ruby seat with a horse head and a music box!), used various oily potions she saw advertised, and herself devoted quite a few blocks of time to sitting with her son in the bathroom to read to him or tell him stories. We had many consultations in which I consistently advised her to shift her focus and lighten her emphasis. She was simply unable or unwilling to do so, however. The result was a very constipated, untrained three-year-old—who will probably suffer from constipation for years to come.

Toilet training was *very* important to this mother— *too* important. Her own needs to have her child succeed at it actually interfered with his own ability to choose to use a toilet. I honestly believe that when it comes to toilet training, "less is more."

One of my mothers well illustrates the effectiveness and ease of the less-is-more policy. She managed to toilet train all four of her children at very different times without any major difficulties. Her first-born, a son, was over 2½ (more about him in a moment). The second child, a daughter who was 17 months younger than the oldest, wanted to do everything he did—and she insisted on toilet training with him. Fortunately, her body somehow was able to cooperate and she was almost entirely potty trained by the time she was one. The third child, another girl, was four years younger and trained by about 18 months. The fourth child was eagerly trained by his much admired brother, Jack, the first-born child.

Jack actually had one traumatic experience with his own toilet training, which could have turned into a developmental set-back if his parents had reacted differently. Jack was just under two years when his mother gave birth to the second child. He had already begun toilet training and was using the method of standing on a step ladder to urinate. After the arrival of his first sibling, he showed some normal signs of regressing, but he was still trying to be a "big boy." One day while his mother was changing the baby's diapers, Jack proudly went into the bathroom to do things the "big-boy way." When he stood up on his little step ladder, it slipped on the bathroom tiles, and he fell into the toilet.

Although Jack suffered no injuries other than sustaining a terrible scare, he wouldn't go near the bathroom for several weeks. His mother and I had one phone conversation about this aversion behavior and she was quite clear that he should be allowed his fear. The fall had been a real trauma for him and she did not want to push the training when he was opposing it. She understood that he was frightened and she *trusted* that after his fear subsided, his natural desire to feel clean and dry would resurface—and it did. I applauded her view and told her she should give classes on the subject! In this accepting and trusting environment, Jack became more secure and started using the potty chair again. Finally he resumed the step ladder method (rubber stoppers had been glued to the legs) without incident.

The consumed parent is more inclined to let the child take the lead in potty training—but for the wrong reasons. The right reasons are recognizing that only the child can let you know when he or she is able, willing, and ready to begin this new learning. More often the case, the consumed parent is so busy feeding the child whenever and whatever is desired, letting him sleep or not sleep as he so chooses, and bribing him to behave on errands, that there is no energy left over for one more task. Sooner or later the child realizes that sitting on the toilet is yet another tool in his storehouse of manipulations that can be used to wield power over parents.

For many a beleaguered parent, the impetus to potty train comes from the simple, human desire to *not* change diapers. All of us vary in our tolerance levels for these areas of personal hygiene. Some parents are simply unable to clean up vomit without vomiting themselves. Others do it with *relative* ease. Parents with low tolerances will naturally be inclined to introduce toilet training quite early. That's fine, as long as the child's cues are quickly followed and *respected*. If training fails, don't blame yourself or your child. Recognize your need as a valid one, and then be prepared to keep changing the diapers.

The *idea* of using a toilet can be introduced at one-and-a-half years of age. You might show your child the training potty and say, "I want you to make your poop in the potty." If your child brings you his poop in his keds, you know he hasn't understood! Children vary enormously in their cognitive grasp of this concept. They may be very "bright" in other areas but slow in this one. That is why the actual initiative to use a toilet must come from the child. When the child begins cuing you in any way that she is aware of her body functionings, you can begin to offer her the possibility of using the toilet. The moment you use bribery to get the child on the toilet—or punishment in response to accidents—you are nudging toilet training into a special category that could cause special problems not too far down the road.

Parents can easily become too identified with the issue of toilet training. If their child does not understand by 15 months or 18 months, parents think it means they must be doing something wrong—or, worse, that the child must be lacking in intelligence. In reality, age of toilet training has nothing whatsoever to do with level of intelligence. Another common response for parents is to feel embarrassed and ashamed if their child isn't trained by two or two-and-a-half. I realize there may be complicated emotional and psychological issues that generate these feelings of embarrassment and shame, and I encourage my parents to determine if professional counseling would be desirable. Any shame they feel is going to be communicated to the child, and that is both unfair to the child and counterproductive to their goals.

Ultimately, take relief in knowing that siblings as well as peer influence can also play a significant role in helping your child become toilet trained. It's not all up to you. The first-born usually starts later and takes longer to train than siblings simply because he or she has no role model to follow—unless the child is in a pre-school. Most pre-schools, unfortunately, will not take young children who are not toilet trained, so that usually leaves the first-born without exposure to peers.

I had some notions of changing this policy when I first opened my nursery school in 1972. I used the kibbutz principle in structuring our bathroom set-up. Israeli kibbutzs are known for their highly successful methods of toilet training: as befitting a communal environment, all the toddlers and young children line up in a row and use the open toilets *en masse* at the same time. They learn in the most natural way possible—from one another.

In my school many small potties were lined up in a row, a few feet apart, all open. Often, an untrained child would learn to use the potty out of a simple desire to socialize with a child who was already making use of it. The untrained child would sit and talk to the trained child, and soon the untrained child would be success-fully imitating his companion. The learning would be effortless, free of bribery, and devoid of whistles and bangles. Potty training became a shared experience among peers rather than an endless source of aggravation, nagging, and crying.

The most important point to understand is that, unless a child is brain-damaged or has some organic impairment, he or she *will* become toilet trained—that's a guarantee. The less fuss and emotion surrounding the topic, the better. Lighten up about it, use humor, use laughter. In a class on discipline I gave recently for parents of newborns through three-year-olds, out of 90 participants, the second most common question concerned how or when to toilet train (the first was on discipline). My last admonition on this subject was to "just back off for a while—don't do any training but keep them in training pants, and see what happens."

In a follow-up meeting a couple of months later, half of the parents with children between two and three who had "backed off" reported that their kids had actually indicated their own desire to begin using the potty. It was remarkable to me! Kids will learn in their own time in such a painless way. You don't have to orchestrate anything.

℞

Prescription for Winning at Potty Training

1. Do not overemphasize potty training and **never use bribery or cajolery**.

2. Avoid the "comparison mentality."

3. Keep in mind the three basic ingredients of potty training to determine your child's readiness and ability.

4. Keep the teaching process simple; avoid the "whistles and bangles" of elaborate techniques.

5. Remember that "less is more" when it comes to training.

6. Let the initiative to use the toilet come from your child.

7. Remember that your child's readiness to potty train is not related to his or her level of intelligence!

8. Allow potty-trained siblings and peers to set a natural example for your child.

9. Remember that every adult you know is potty-trained!

8 ❧

Letting Go
With Grace

*A child's separation anxiety does not originate
in the child, but within the parents who have
too much fear to trust new situations.*

I believe in preschool. I even advocate preschool. I
think it's the greatest invention for mothers since the
washing machine. And the really superlative point is
that it benefits the child as well as the mother—provided
the mother is willing to allow it and even foster it.

Children are like houseplants: from time to time,
they need to be uprooted and placed in a larger environment. Preschool can be likened to an environmental
re-potting of your young child. Without this regular
adjustment of growing space, children—like plants—
will become root-bound, house-bound. . .and so will
their mothers.

Each stage of infancy and childhood has a parallel
stage of learning and development for the parent. When

the baby is first born, the parent's task is to learn to perceive and interpret the cues and the needs of the baby. By the toddler stage, the parent's task changes as the child's autonomy blossoms; now the parent must learn to accept some loss of control for the first time, while maintaining necessary limits. Once the child reaches preschool age, the parent is faced with the full-blown challenge of learning to separate—and that is rarely an easy learning.

These stages of infancy and childhood are also characterized by what I call the "Decline of Influence Curve."

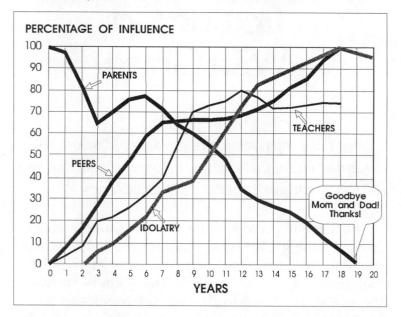

From birth until about 18 months, the parent is the biggest influence in the child's life. By 18 months the peer group begins to impact the child as she plays in the park or attends "Mommy and Me" classes. If the child is in preschool by the time she is three, peers and teachers will play an increasing part in the child's development. Frankly, I think parental influence peaks when the child is five and enters a dip forever after. By the time the child is eight, you've got stronger peer influence and the addition of media and its step-child, idolatry. You may want to tear your hair out watching your eight-year-old daughter and her playmate imitating Madonna, but the brutal fact is, you can't compete with Madonna. What you can do is understand that the never-ending encroachment on your parental influence is completely normal and ideally leads to your child's emergence into mature adulthood. Rather than fight Madonna and your dwindling influence with rigid rules, look for the best ways to facilitate your child's outreaches to the larger world. Accept the "Decline of Influence Curve" as an indication that your child is doing exactly what he or she is supposed to be doing: developing into a self-determining individual who knows how to set limits.

The first separation of preschool is perhaps most difficult for the mother, assuming that she has been the primary caretaker of the child. She has grown accustomed to having a great deal of control over her child's environment and what he is exposed to. She is used to being the center of the child's life and she is used to having the child be the center of her life. This is especially true for mothers who have the choice of being full-time moms. Mothers who return to work within a year after delivery have already grappled with separation. When working is a *must* for the mother, separation is made easier—simply because she doesn't have the luxury of choosing. If the child doesn't like preschool in the beginning, the working mother does not have the choice of whether or not to take the child out of school. The working mom can change the preschool, but she cannot choose to quit working and keep her child at home. Since most children will adjust to anything that gives them fun, the working mother is forced to wait out the difficult adjustment period—when there is one, which there isn't necessarily—whereas the non-working mother can choose to withdraw her child from preschool, believing that her child must not be ready.

I always remind my non-working mothers that children need time to adjust to the new—just like adults also need time. I don't know of any "grown-up" who changes jobs or goes back to school without enduring a certain amount of discomfort in the initial stages.

Each age group has its own kind of learning and socialization. One of my mothers actually believed that it was better for her child to stay home then to go to preschool because she was always worried that he would "catch something" from other kids (more on germs later). When he finally began kindergarten, it was instant disaster. The first day he walked over to a child who was riding a tricycle and pushed him off screaming, "It's *mine!*" In this child's little world of Mommy and Me, everything *was* his. Instead of letting her child learn how to share by interacting with his peers, the mother assumed the teacher had not done her job of protecting her child by giving him whatever he wanted. She pulled him out of the school, attacking it as "undisciplined" (who's really undisciplined in this story?) and began a futile search for a "more enlightened" school.

A young child needs to learn from her peers, not just from adults. A child needs to learn how the world is experienced from a *child's* point of view—which the parent can't begin to know. Separation and socialization usually go hand-in-hand. As a child learns to separate from her parents, she learns to socialize with her peers; and in this process, she learns about structure and boundaries. Prior to preschool, boundaries have been set by two parents and enforced in a relatively small space (the home). When the child enters preschool for the first time, she moves into a far more complex environment of structure and boundaries—but within a framework of fun and play—that prepares her for grade school.

Separation and the Consumed/ Consuming Cycle

The challenge of separation evokes different patterns of response for consuming and consumed parents.

Whether I am the mother who is consumed by child or the mother who is consuming the child, either way, I'm going to have a difficult time separating—because in both cases there is an over-identification with the child that will spawn conflicts and anxieties.

The consuming parent is never ready for separation and there will never be a school that is good enough. The consuming parent is accustomed to manipulating the child, to directing most of the child's activities, to focusing exclusively on the child. Preschool requires that the parent move out of the position as primary caretaker to one in which she has far less control and far more competition in the form of other children and teachers— and the consuming parent does not find it easy to give up all that control.

If you are used to shielding your child from any possible discomfort, you will find the thought of preschool to be a threatening one, indeed. There are so many variables that are completely outside your control that *could* impinge upon your child. As a parent you want to make the road your child has to trod as smooth as possible. That is natural. But if you are caught in a consuming mode of parenting, then you are futilely attempting to make the road so smooth it's unnatural. No matter how hard we as parents try to shield our children from pain, some of the pain has to happen— because if it doesn't, then the child never learns how to cope with unpleasant or difficult feelings. In order to develop into adults who have resources to draw upon, the child needs prior experiences of coping: of having a bad feeling, sitting with it, finding out that the world doesn't end, and then maybe even finding some of her own solutions. That's how you build character. Over-protecting a child, however well-intentioned, robs her of these valuable experiences that create a selfhood.

My own mother certainly had her moments of over-protection, but what stands out in my memory are the times when she stood back and let me experience something difficult. I remember a time in the eighth grade when I had gone from well-built to chubby. When it came time to pick the football team, Kent Huggins, who was captain of the team, didn't pick me. I didn't understand why I had been overlooked, so I asked.

He answered simply, "Because you're fat."

I went home to my room, closed the door, and turned off the lights. I didn't go to dinner (and I was typically on time for food). My mother found me sitting on my bed, lights out, with my head down. All she asked was, "Are you going to feel this way tomorrow?" I said, "Well, no." Turning to leave she said, "Well, why don't you just think about how you're going to feel tomorrow." The next day I was fine—I didn't want to continue to feel miserable, but my mother had given me the autonomy to do so—which helped me to choose otherwise.

The consumed parent is accustomed to being manipulated by the child, to letting the child dictate her life, to catering to the child's demands and whims. She is so invested in making sure the child's needs are met that all sense of *personhood* is lost. The child demands and receives her total focus, and even though it runs her ragged, she is used to it. Losing that exclusive focus can leave an uncomfortable gap in the parent's life.

The child of the consumed parent also won't let go: he's got a good thing here, and he knows it. Why go off to some foreign environment where he doesn't wield the kind of power he does at home? On a good day the consumed parent is fed up with being run ragged and realizes preschool might be a good idea. Now she is stricken with guilt because she *wants* her child to go to preschool. She feels like she's trying to get rid of him— and she is, for a few hours a day!

The Right Way to Separate

Parents who do not put their children in school until they are five or six are depriving them of a confirming, consolidating view of the world. The child who finds himself in school for the first time at age five, and who has not had a lot of contact with other children, may manifest a number of behavioral problems ranging from belligerence (as in our example above) to phobic responses of aversion and fear. The experience of being separated from parents is so unfamiliar, and the pattern of living under their surveillance and protection so entrenched, that the first move away from home is a wrenching one.

Growthful separation involves two equally important factors: the child's readiness for separation and the parent's willingness to separate. It is the most natural thing in the world for kids to want to play with others who are their same size. They are supposed to develop less interest in you as a parent and more interest in their peer group. They are supposed to learn how to ride the tricycle with their peer group, not with you. You certainly can share these moments—the slide, the swing, the teeter-totter. But for the most part, I think the children themselves prefer to share new activities with their peers.

By and large, most children are ready and eager to explore the worlds beyond their home—unless they pick up fear or ambivalence in one or both parents. Kids can sense, like animals, when the parent doesn't want to let go. *A child's separation anxiety does not originate in the child, but within the parents who have too much fear to trust new situations.* Children learn reticence and a lack of openness to the new from their parents; they learn to be guarded because their parents present a very guarded front about any new environment.

In my preschool I witnessed a mother acting out her unwillingness to let go of her child in a manner that was a crystal-clear enactment of my above point. I couldn't have planned or written a better scene, even if I'd tried. I happened to be in the area of the parking lot when this mother was dropping off her child for the first day of preschool. *The child* was one happy streak as he plunged toward his new world. One step behind, trying to keep up, *the mother* was yelling, "I love you...I'll be back in a little while...don't worry...don't miss me too much...I love you!" She was able to catch hold of his sleeve to

beseech him not to miss her too much, but she didn't even get to finish the sentence—so eager was this child to be on his way.

This scenario is often continued at home. Now the child has been at school for the day, he comes home with a smile on his face, and the parent, in all honesty, feels a pang of jealously, a pang of, *How could I be replaced that easily?* Confused by how she feels, the parent might ask, "Did you miss me?" "Did you have any problems?" Even: "How did you get along without me?" Such questions communicate a veiled but potent double message to the child. On some level the child is hearing: *Succeed at school, but miss me terribly...Make friends, but don't...Be happy...but have a bad time.*

This is a case of "Is the glass half *empty* or half *full?*" Does the parent see preschool as a threatening or enhancing experience? When the parent is willing to let go, her questions will implicitly affirm the day's events:

"Did you have a good time?"

"Did you make any new friends?"

"Did you like the games you played?"

Even if the child answers "No" to each question, the parent can help the child develop a positive expectation about "tomorrow," or pursue *why* the child didn't make any new friends or why the playing wasn't fun. The parent who is unwilling to let go will look for a scapegoat (the school, the teacher, the other children) to explain her child's discomfort. The parent who is willing to foster this new stage of separation will eschew scapegoating and look for ways to help the child adjust comfortably.

At the other end of the continuum is the parent who is so concerned about placing the child in the "best" preschool possible, the child's own needs are overlooked in the process. Here, the mother's anxiety over separation is diverted (Freud would say *sublimated,* I think) into the task of uncovering a place good enough to become a caretaker of her child.

One of my mothers brought in her three-year-old complaining of a terrible stomach ache. He was seen twice in one week. I examined him, did a blood panel, checked for appendicitis, checked for a bowel obstruction—and found nothing wrong anywhere. The third office visit took place about 10:30 in the morning. I asked the mother if he was in preschool and she said, "No, not yet. Actually, we're in the process of interviewing. He has an interview later this morning—it's his fourth one in a week."

I told her that was child abuse. Fortunately, we had a good enough relationship for her to absorb my comment without falling apart. She was upset but relieved to have identified the source of her son's severe stomach aches. Her response was, "I don't know what to do. We want to get him into the finest nursery school, and this is what some of them require." I told her no preschool worth its reputation should have such a requirement in the first place. I think it should happen in the reverse: Parents should be interviewing the nursery-school staffs to see if *they* are acceptable!

The mother canceled the upcoming interview.

Sometimes, as in the above case, the child is ready to let go, but the environment is not the right one. Perhaps the parents are not ready yet and thus go in search of the impossible—the perfect preschool. Unfortunately, their notion of perfect includes a standard of education that is absurd and unnecessary for the young child, whose most pressing needs should be having fun. First grade is time enough to be saddled with academic endeavors. Children who are put in high-pressured, overly scholastic preschools are "burnt out" by the time they are four! I'm not exaggerating. I've seen "childhood burn-out" in my office on many occasions.

Don't assume your child is having trouble adjusting to preschool because he or she is emotionally unable to separate from you. When a child is unhappy in preschool, I think it is usually a problem with the environment, not with the child. In your concern over some adjustment difficulty, try not to jump to the conclusion that your child is not ready. Investigate the environment—the teacher, the physical set-up, your child's peers—and consider a preschool with a different approach before retreating from this new world entirely.

Choice and Timing

The new environment—the first environment to nurture separation—has to be *safe* and *fun*. There isn't one of us who doesn't respond better to something that is fun than something that is work. Some educational skills can be involved—learning sounds, textures, colors—but the primary goal is to foster and facilitate enjoyable, playful socialization. When it's fun, it's easy to adapt. When children learn how to be socially well-adjusted, at ease, confident in preschool, a whole area of anxiety that can block later learning is eliminated.

If you have any conscious control in the matter, do not time the beginning of preschool with the arrival of a new baby. It looks to the child like, "The new car is coming in so you get rid of the old one." Ideally, place your child in preschool two or three months before or after the new baby comes—preferably *before*, so that the child already has his new world established before having to adapt to a sibling. Preschool is a marvelous counterbalance to the shock of displacement, especially for the firstborn. The experience automatically expands the child's horizons, even at a time when he wishes he were the only child on the planet—or at least in *his* home.

In deciding when to enroll your child in preschool, the bottom line is that *there is no general rule*. Some children are not ready at age three; others are raring to go at age two. The trick is to be sure your own fears of separation are not influencing your child. More often than not, the three-year-old who is terrified of preschool has experienced some degree of overprotectiveness and would benefit from a gentle introduction to a peer-group activity.

In their efforts to be responsibly protective, parents often have the tendency to focus on a particular quality or behavior and label it as the reason their child is not ready for preschool. "Billy is extremely shy—he still clings to me in public places." "Jody doesn't mix well with children in the park." "Rusty is too boisterous and hyper." In my experience, most children two or older can gain a tremendous amount from attending preschool. Children who tend to cling are ready; children who are boisterous and hyperactive are ready; children who are highly introverted are ready—provided it's the right school and the parents are genuinely supportive and enthusiastic.

I watched one set of parents reverse this pattern of using problem areas as a reason to keep a child out of preschool. Instead, they used the preschool to *treat* the problem. Their two-and-a-half-year-old daughter had never spoken to anyone but them. She would not talk to her peers, she would not talk to relatives, she would not talk to me or to anyone in our office. Since there was nothing abnormal in her behavior—no signs of anxiety or stress—her parents had not taken her for psychological or speech therapy evaluations. However, they did decide to put her in preschool. The teacher was convinced the child had a major problem (that thought had definitely crossed our minds, as well), but the director of the school believed that the child simply needed to adjust in her own time. His perspective was, "Let's just let her handle this in her own way—she'll come around." It took six months, but by the end of that time period, the little girl had become a chatterbox—first with her peers, and then with adults.

This is not to say that preschool is a panacea, by any means. It is, however, a tremendous resource that can be tapped.

Mothers often ask how many hours a week should the child be in preschool? In most cases my answer is, "As many hours as your child can tolerate." The more continuity, the better. Attending preschool two mornings a week can be more difficult for the child than attending on a daily basis, simply because the two-day-a-week child is not in the new environment long enough or often enough to get used to it, to make it his own, to set down roots, so to speak. His primary focus remains at home, because that is where he experiences the most continuity in his world.

Children are naturally inquisitive and gutsy. They are also inveterate imitators; they socialize by copying. The timid three-year-old who is afraid of the slide or the swings in the park is going to want to imitate his classmate in preschool who is not afraid—unless an adult scares him with warnings that he may fall and hurt himself. Children are one another's best teachers—and I really do believe that they get more out of life by being with their peers than by being with adults.

What About Germs?

Recently I watched a late-night episode of *I Love Lucy* and was bemused to find that the story revolved around the topic of the chapter I was working on: Lucy's inability to let "Little Ricky" start nursery school. Father Ricky was all in favor of his son taking his first independent step, but Lucy was distraught at the prospect. For one thing, Little Ricky would be exposed to "all those colds and runny noses." In the course of the half-hour episode, every theme I have discussed in this chapter was humorously touched upon—including Lucy's manipulative questioning of Little Ricky before his first day at school: Something to the effect of, "You don't want to go to that dirty old school with all those bullies, do you, honey?" Put the question together with Lucy shaking her head as she peers at her young son with huge doe-eyes, and no one is surprised when Little Ricky dutifully answers, "No, Mommy."

At Ricky's insistence, Little Ricky goes anyway. When he becomes ill with tonsillitis within the first week of attending nursery school, Lucy launches into a plaintive "I-told-you-so" speech in which she accuses the nursery school and all its children of making her baby sick. Her doctor then calmly reminds her that Little Ricky had periodic bouts of tonsillitis long before he ever came near a preschool. In the end, both Little Ricky and Lucy adjust to his new part-time life away from her.

In any episode, Lucy's appeal comes from the fact that she is usually "right on" in portraying some common aspect of our lives. In this particular episode, most parents can share in Lucy's terror to one degree or another, though few would act it out so hilariously, as she did. Nonetheless, preschool looms in the distance, a specter of germs and difficult adjustments for your child. The larger picture, however, is that sooner or later your child will have to enter social groups. The new preschooler has a virgin immune system and it, too, gets "educated" by being exposed to a host of new stimuli. I'm not saying that you have to like the increase in colds, but I am saying that it is undesirable to keep a child out of pre-school because of your fear of germs. Unless you intend to keep your child at home—in a bubble—for the next 15 years or so, sooner or later his immune system is going to have to be introduced to the Troops of the outside world.

If your child is able to participate in school activities even with a cold (runny nose but *no fever*), I feel that it is fine to send her. The idea that you are exposing "well" children to your child's cold is a weak rationalization—anytime you take your child into a supermarket or to a public park, you are running almost the same risk.

Although preschool initially offers the child increased exposure to common germs of various sorts, it also offers the not-so-common gift of identity, self-confidence, and the first seeds of independence.

Because infants and children are highly needy and non-self-caring, parents quickly become attached to and even dependent on fulfilling those needs. It makes us *feel good* to fulfill needs, to help. In this process the ability to differentiate our own needs as parents and caretakers from those of our children can become blurred. What makes us feel good and secure may not always be what is optimal for our children.

As parents we need to teach our children how to separate from us, how to begin shaping their own autonomy and individuality. The reason some families find their 20-year-olds still lurking around the house with no idea of what to do with their lives is partly because those kids do not know how to separate. Their thinking is, "Why should I go live in a dormitory when my mother cooks my meals and does my laundry at home?" On a deeper level most of these kids are also afraid of taking that step, of severing the tie.

Young people who are unable to push away the inappropriate portions of society that lure them into drugs and excessive behavior are young people who have not exercised their ability to make independent decisions. The beginnings of being able to say no to drugs at the age of 12 or 15, or to make sensible, responsible judgments and to join the world as a true individual at 18, can be found in this first milestone experience when you *un*clasp your child's hand and send him or her off to preschool.

℞

Prescription for Winning at Separating

1. Remember that separating from your child is as much a learning process for you as it is for the child.

2. Take a positive attitude toward the "Decline of Influence Curve."

3. Learn to value peer influence; remember that a child needs to learn how the world is experienced from a *child's* point of view.

4. Try to remember that separation ultimately enhances your child's developing selfhood as well as your own, probably flagging, sense of personhood.

5. Introduce your child (and yourself) to the experience of separating by enrolling him or her in preschool. Don't wait for kindergarten to begin this inevitable process.

6. Bear in mind that, generally, your child's separation anxieties originate in your own fears and lack of trust in new situations. Communicate trust.

7. Also remember that, if you are genuinely willing to foster this new stage of separation, you will eschew scapegoating when problems arise in the process and look for ways to help your child adjust comfortably.

8. Avoid the pitfall of searching for the "perfect preschool"—the Harvard for toddlers. Preschool is for *fun*, not academics.

9 ❦

"I'll Show You Mine, If You'll Show Me Yours"

Just as a child cannot learn much about healthy eating in an eat-and-run, grab-and-snack family, neither can he or she learn about healthy sex in a home where the expression of love and affection is rare or non-existent.

Sexuality is partly inborn. If we could only learn to accept the fact that children are sexual beings from crib to college, we would not be so frightened by the overt sexuality that appears in the 11-to-15-year age group.

Sexuality is also partly learned. Although parents would like to believe that they are solely responsible for what their children learn about sex, there are many uncontrollable influences ranging from the child's peers to MTV music videos. Parents can finally win the upper hand not by dictatorial diatribes and repressive attitudes, but by providing *explicit patterns of consistent behavior* that demonstrate a loving and affectionate interaction between them as spouses. The structure that will ultimately house all of your child's attitudes and values on sex and loving will be of his or her own unique design; but the foundation on which it rests can be one of your making—one that radiates a willing exchange of affection, trust, intimacy, and commitment between two people in partnership.

How children experience their sexuality will be influenced by the degree of comfort or discomfort with which their parents experience their own sexuality. When parents keep their affections for one another behind locked doors, it can foster sexual confusion in their children; sex becomes dissociated and compartmentalized. We all know that sex isn't just about the penis and the vagina—that's intercourse. *Sexuality,* however, is a relational experience comprised of emotions, passions, feelings, and values. Affection is a form of foreplay. Kids who see affection freely and frequently flow between their parents learn in a subtle way to see sex as more than the act—because they are seeing it as part of the seamless whole that is their parents' relationship.

If we as parents want our children to grow into loving human beings, *they must first experience and recognize the loving that takes place in their homes.* We are responsible for letting our children know that kissing and hugging are just as much a part of the life we are sharing with them as eating, sleeping, and playing. Above all, we must realize that just as our children have their own individual appetites, sleep requirements, and play preferences, so do they have *their own* sexual feelings.

Real sex education involves sharing the *who, what, why, and when* of loving feelings and lovemaking in the day-to-day family environment. If we can imagine the reasonable placement of life's activities within the framework of our days, we will see the evolvement of sex just as we observe a baby progress from a diet of mashed bananas to whole fruit. Although we cannot determine or control when a child will openly request instruction, we *can* openly demonstrate healthy and loving sexual attitudes within the child's range of observation. Just as a child cannot learn much about healthy eating in an eat-and-run, grab-and-snack family, neither can he or she learn about healthy sex in a home where the expression of love and affection is rare or non-existent.

Keep Your Answers Simple

As a rule of thumb, allow your child to initiate questions about sexuality rather than announcing a parental lecture on the subject. As your child's verbal skills develop, keep open to cues indicating sexual concerns. Some children will want to ask questions from age two on, while others will not show any interest until nine or ten years of age. Usually, there is no single identifiable moment or day when your child lights up with his or her first flush of sexual interest. It is a subtle process that varies with each child.

Information about sex must be prudently delivered, not dumped in large amounts. Would you feed your child a year's supply of vegetables at one sitting just because they are good for him? Like food, sexual information must be offered in small and nutritive portions if it is to be successfully digested.

Always consider the age and attention-span of the child who is asking the question and be careful to determine what it is he wants to know. If a three-year-old asks, "Where did I come from?", he may be wondering which hospital rather than which part of the anatomy. Question him a bit to figure out what direction he is heading and then keep your answer straightforward and simple. Answering a five-year-old's queries about the differences between boys and girls with a comprehensive explanation of anatomy, physiology, endocrinology, and procreative processes would be like giving him the year's supply of vegetables at once. He doesn't need it all at once. He needs it parcelled out.

Children are very literal—more literal than we tend to remember. If you answer your four-year-old's question about where he came from by telling him that Daddy has a tool that spreads seeds into Mommy's field, you may find your child hunting through the garage in search of his own tool and seeds.

There are several excellent books available to help you with this inevitable task. My favorite is *Where Do I Come From?* by Peter Mayle because it is simple and visual. It makes the parent's job of explaining all that much easier. This is a valuable educational aid for parents that uses people—not rabbits, cows or dogs—to explain human sexuality. Another alternative is to leave these kinds of books lying around, available. Your child's own curiosity will then determine when the subject is explored.

Unfortunately, mothers are more likely to be asked questions first, simply because they have more exposure to the child than the fathers. If you feel comfortable answering, do so; if not, tell your child you'll explain it to her later, and then enlist the help of your husband.

As parents you can certainly anticipate the questions your child will invariably ask at some point. Before this time comes, talk to one another about how you want to answer; talk about any "hang-ups" you may be feeling. Know that your answer will be colored by whatever attitudes are beneath the surface: be they attitudes of discomfort and embarrassment or ones of honesty, comfort, and willingness to share. Your answer will also be colored by your "definition" of sex: If you believe that sex is primarily an anatomical experience, then your child will inherit this view. If, on the other hand, you have experienced sex as a multifaceted exchange between two people in relationship, then your child will assimilate this more multidimensional perspective.

Children learn about sex as they grow; sex education occurs in a developmental framework. As children grow older, the more they will want to know. I stress the importance of emphasizing the relational aspect of sex from the very beginning. Find a way to talk about *feelings* as well as anatomy, even to your three-year-old. When I was trying to teach my kids about sex, I discussed very little anatomy. I talked about sex as something that included friendship and good feelings and touching.

Despite the best of answers from parents, children may still be more influenced by their peers, whose answers are often questionable, at best! The following letter is from an eight-year-old patient, Kevin, who was asked to write down what he knew about sex. I am well acquainted with this child's parents and know that they have answered whatever questions he has asked in an open and honest manner. Yet, the information Kevin reports comes from his friend "Mark"—not from Mom or Dad:

Sex!

1. Mark Goldberg told me that groin is a part of sex. 2. And he told me about the boos, on a ladys upper parts of the stomace. 3. And he also told me about the but.

Answers

1. Groin is two tubes connected two your balls. One is red and one is green. And one holds your shit and one holds your pee.
2. Boobs are big round things. they are only on a girls stomace but Males have little ones.
3. And the but is two round fat things. Females and males have them

Sex

1. Mark goldberg told me that groin is a part of sex. And he told me about the boos, on a ladys upper parts of the stomace. And he also told me about the but.

Answers

1. Groin is two tubes connected two your balls. One is red and one is green. And one holds your shit and one holds your pee.
2. Boobs are big round things. they are only on a girls stomace but Males have little ones.
3. And the but is two round fat things. Females and males both have them

Isn't that marvelous! What happens to the information we provide? Apparently, it is repeated to peers and, like the game of Telephone, it is hardly recognizable at the end of the line. The children chew it up, toss it around, dissect it, and merge it until it easily accommodates their own level of understanding.

Don't be discouraged if, after all your careful "education," your child comes home from school with a four-letter word for sexual intercourse. In all likelihood, the child is not discounting what was learned at home but is simply striving to be "in." The child is also testing you. Using swear words in a large group or asking how you feel about "blow jobs" while you're in the supermarket is a way of testing whether your reactions are congruent with the information you have been giving—or whether, underneath it all, you are really "uptight" and disapproving. Proceed with caution and lightheartedness!

From Freudian Repression to Nudity in the Home in a Decade!

We are all aware of the fact that there is a tremendous difference in a sexual attitudes between today's parents and those of 30 years ago. The sexual liberation that emerged during the 1960s was an overt demonstration by our young people that they did not agree with their parents' value structures. As they moved to create structures more reflective of their new attitudes and beliefs, the pendulum swung wide from the weight and momentum of change: from repression to shockingly full expression in which promiscuity was reframed as freedom. At the very least the sixties brought us a new attitude—that the body is natural and beautiful—that has helped a large segment of our society come out of the Dark Ages. But I think it is an attitude that also can be carried too far. In their desire to bequeath open and uninhibited sexual attitudes to their children, "modern" parents can lose all sight of appropriate boundaries and healthy lines of privacy. I've had parents ask me if it's okay for their four-year-old daughter to touch her father's penis in the shower. I wondered, If it was okay for the little girl to touch her father's penis in the shower, is it also okay for the little boy to touch his mother's vagina in the shower?

How far do we take the permissive attitude? How far do we take the new directive, "The body is beautiful and should not be hidden?" How do parents draw a line that denotes a simple boundary of privacy rather than a barbed wire of shame and repression? My feeling is, if you're asking if some action or behavior is acceptable, then you've got some doubt and discomfort about it—which means you probably should make some changes.

Casual Nudity. Another question I've been asked is, "How much nudity should be allowed in the home? Is it okay to be nude in front of our young children?" My answer is: Nudity is a problem only for those who are uncomfortable with it but do it anyway because they think it is in vogue or because they believe it will liberate their children of all future sexual and bodily hang-ups. Such nudity has a heavy agenda attached to it that will inevitably be confusing for the child. The mother who is often nude in front of her eight-year-old son must expect that one day he could walk up and playfully touch her nipples or stroke her pubic hair. Nudity provides a level of stimulation that no one—especially the child—is equipped to deal with. Repeated nudity, I think, is unnecessarily provocative and may produce later feelings of guilt and shame in a child who recognizes that he or she experienced sexual feelings in relation to a parent. This is contrasted by the casual nudity experienced in large families raised in small farm houses, for example, where family members inevitably bump into each other going into and out of the one bathroom. Here, young children have an experience of occasionally seeing a parent nude, but there is no "baggage" attached it—in the farm context, it is about as unusual as a sunrise.

Masturbation. What do you do when two-year-old boy walks around playing with himself? What do you do when your five-year-old daughter plants herself spread-eagle in front of the warm water outlets in the swimming pool six times a day? These (or variations thereof) are commonly asked questions in my pediatric discussions with parents.

In my childhood days, masturbation raised the thunderous threat of damnation and/or blindness. Nowadays, our overall attitudes have changed markedly, though there is still a surprising amount of embarrassment and shame surrounding the topic of masturbation. Today's parents (in general) do not want to punish masturbation, as our grandparents and even parents did. But they do want to set some healthy parameters. You want your child to feel good about his or her body, and you also want your child to understand about *privacy*. I typically suggest that parents tell their children that touching themselves doesn't belong in the public eye. You want to call the least amount of attention to whatever the child is doing, because the more attention you call to something, the more the child will want to do it. If your child initiates self-stimulation in a social situation—say, at a group picnic on a Saturday afternoon in the park—just find an easy way to distract her. Fortunately, most children are easily distractible.

To parents who find their children's self-stimulating explorations to be embarrassing or even "horrifying" (one mother was extremely upset by it), I recommend that they begin to talk about their own sexual hang-ups with friends, spouse, or a professional. Masturbating is all part of growing up; it's all part of one's sexuality. Teaching your child to enjoy her own body inevitably involves allowing her to explore and touch. Set the neutral boundaries of privacy around the behavior without imparting the stinging arrows of shame and embarrassment.

I'll Show You Mine If You'll Show Me Yours. What about children exploring each other's bodies? That, too, is almost inevitable—and usually healthy, assuming the children are about the same age. Discrepancies in age suggest inequalities that all too easily render one child power over another. You do not want to allow that. If, however, you walk into a room and find two three-year-old toddlers giggling and rolling around with most of their clothes off, *do not* gasp in shock and horror and ask in an accusatory tone, "*What* are you two *doing*???" Instead, you might say casually, "Time to put our clothes back on," and begin helping them dress. If you communicate an attitude that it's okay to look and to touch, children will quickly get bored and move on to other activities.

Children learn by imitating and experimenting. One of my patients, Rachel, age three, was upstairs playing with three of her friends (all around the same age) and the parents were downstairs visiting. Rachel's mother came upstairs to check on everyone and, standing outside the open doorway, observed her daughter say with great authority to the little boy, "I'm Dr. Buddy, pull down your pants." The mother responded by stifling her laughter and coolly collecting the kids to watch television. Once they were installed in the den, she phoned me with the anecdote and we laughed uproariously.

Children hear these directions in our offices all the time. "Take off your shirt," "Slide down your pants," "Take off your dress." Here is Rachel, dutifully imitating her pediatrician as a way of staging her own explorations and getting straight to the interesting part of the examination—the part she hasn't seen.

If you give kids the opportunity to explore, they are going to explore. If you are concerned about this kind of behavior, another alternative is to not leave children alone in, say, the upstairs bedroom for hours on end; don't put them down for naps together.

Toddler Explorations. What about children exploring their parents' bodies? I don't recommend it past infancy. Infants will naturally touch their mothers; this age is about stroking, touching, and caressing. However, if a two-year-old is sitting on his mother's lap and caressing her nipples through her blouse, I don't think that should be allowed. The mother can casually move the child's hand, distract him, play with his fingers. Daughters bouncing on their fathers' laps past the age of five or so can also be a cause for concern—especially when the behavior continues through adolescence and into the teenage years (I've witnessed 16-year-old, fully developed daughters sitting on their fathers' laps on bus trips to football games). As parents you want your children to grow up being comfortable with their bodies, but you don't want to foster a sexual bond with you by allowing inappropriate exploration. One of my mother's, I discovered, had developed a very inappropriate way of giving comfort to her infant son. Whenever the baby cried, the mother leaned down and blew on his penis—and the baby would stop crying. To my shock, I saw it happen in the examining room one day. I had to take blood from the baby and he began screaming, whereupon his mother bent down, picked up his penis, and blew on it! I suggested that she find another way to comfort her son. She wasn't embarrassed by it—for her, it was an effective method of stopping his crying.

Parental Sex. As I stated in the beginning of this chapter, I believe that children acquire healthy attitudes toward sex by observing parents freely showing affection for one another. However, I do not think it is wise to expose the child to explicit and stimulating sexual behavior. Another legacy from the sixties was to think it was just fine if your child saw you making love. Now, I know there aren't two parents alive who have not had there toddler or young child walk in on them during lovemaking. Such accidents will happen, but they should not be casually encouraged or allowed. I don't think a three-year-old is comfortable being exposed to that level of sexual energy. How does she or he know what to do with it?

My view is that, along with cultivating healthy attitudes toward sex and their own bodies in your children, you can also cultivate a healthy appreciation for *privacy*—yours *and* theirs. I remember a couple who were having a real problem in their sex life. As working parents they were both too tired to make love at night, so a marriage counselor suggested that they make love in the morning. One morning the mother looked over the father's shoulder while they were making love. To her shock, their three-year-old son was sitting on the end of their bed holding a coloring book. They said it took them three months to recover!

One way of answering when you do "get caught" making love, and your privacy has been interrupted, is to say that "Daddy is rocking Mommy to sleep." Rocking is something toddlers and young children understand; it is familiar and comforting. I don't think most children this age really understand what it means to "have sex" or "make love"; therefore, those phrases don't necessarily help clarify the situation.

I knew a couple who were prolific lovemakers. They relied on the explanation of "Daddy is rocking Mommy" countless times; their living quarters were small and they had often been interrupted at inopportune moments. Their little girl, who was four and a half years old when I knew her, was quite pleased to tell me (and many other people) how much Daddy rocked Mommy. She was comfortable with the explanation because it was communicated by her mother in a robust, positive tone that indirectly expressed a healthy appreciation of sex.

The point is not to withhold sexual information because you feel it should be censored; the point is to *provide information the child can understand and be comfortable with.*

The child who is allowed to walk around during the night is bound to wind up in your bedroom at the wrong time. Boundaries around sleep are absolutely essential, as we discussed in Chapter 6, and also help to establish much needed parameters of privacy. Teaching children the pleasure of privacy yields many dividends ranging from the mundane to the sublime. On the mundane side is the fact that a child's desire for privacy means that the parent gets more privacy. On the sublime side, when a child discovers the pleasure of privacy, she is also discovering the pleasure of her own selfhood, which is a core inner resource for the rest of her life.

Children are by nature uninhibited and their need for privacy doesn't usually emerge until well into grade school. However, *your* need for privacy is with you from the day you bring your first baby home from the hospital. *Respect your needs and find ways to accommodate them.* The toddler who wanders into your room late at night, looking for comfort and wanting to sleep with you, is hard to resist. You naturally feel an incredible warmth when your little child crawls into bed and snuggles into your arms. However, be aware that the child will rapidly develop the habit of sleeping with you, unless you set boundaries. It seems to me that two adults ought to be snuggling in each other's arms at night—and that is hard to do when there is this little body lying between the two of you.

Childhood sexuality is an inescapable and vital part of maturation. It is meant to be shared by parent and child, not taught in school auditoriums to separate classes of boys and girls. Childhood sexuality is about touching; childhood sexuality is about learning.

You are in a position as a parent to pass on a sexual legacy of your own making. Whether you are a person who has enjoyed and valued sexuality from the get-go, or whether you have struggled with it as stressful and anxiety-producing, you can make the choice of finding a way to communicate positive messages about sexuality to your young ones. As I watch today's parents butt up against the kinds of sensitive issues that made our parents' generation blanche and go silent (or redden and threaten), I continue to be awed by this generation's efforts to forge through their own dark areas in order to create a legacy of expressiveness and self-acceptance in their children. And in this amazing process, I have seen parents grow as much as their children.

℞

Prescription for Healthy Parental Legacies

1. Remember that if we as parents want our children to grow into loving human beings, *they must first experience and recognize the loving that takes place in their homes.*

2. Allow your child to initiate questions about sexuality and then *keep your answers simple.*

3. If you are unsure how to answer a question, talk it over with your spouse.

4. If you know you are uncomfortable talking to your child about sex, find a way to deal with your discomfort before you engage your child in an exchange.

5. Prepare yourself for all varieties of peer influence when it comes to this topic.

6. When trying to answer the question, "How permissive should I be?" remember the simple formula that if you're wondering if some action or behavior is acceptable (Is it okay for our five-year-old daughter

to shower with her father?), then you've got some doubt and discomfort about it—which means you probably should make some changes.

7. Regarding masturbation, remember that while you want your child to feel good about his or her body, you also want your child to understand about *privacy*. Allow the masturbation, setting the parameters of privacy.

8. Meanwhile, *do not* call a lot of attention to your child's explorations into self-stimulation. Set parameters in an atmosphere of healthy neutrality.

9. Do not withhold sexual information because you feel it should be censored; however, do not provide information that exceeds the grasp of your child's cognitive and emotional development. The point is to *provide information the child can understand and be comfortable with.*

10 ❧

Coping with "Attention Deficit Hyperactive Disorder"

The most damaging myth surrounding ADHD is the assumption that a child's disruptive behavior results from a lack of parental authority and love. ADHD is not a personal indictment against you as parents and people; rather, it is a treatable and controllable illness.

This is a special chapter for me because it deals with a special problem that was little understood until the last two decades or so. Parents with "problem" children had nowhere to turn for answers that did not incriminate them as the source of the difficulty. Answers were long in coming because the syndrome responsible for the aberrant behavior—now called "Attention Deficit Hyperactive Disorder" (ADHD)—was a complex one that harbored many invisible variables.

No other disorder I have encountered in 28 years of practice as a pediatrician can so consistently destroy the morale of parents and children alike. ADHD leaves parents feeling dashed against the rocks of parenthood, smashed to bits of failure; and it leaves children feeling utterly worthless and hopeless, adrift in an ocean without any tools to navigate. Working with parents and ADHD children provided a "baptism by fire" for me. Shocked by the amount of pain and havoc the disorder inflicted, I scrambled to find concrete ways to help.

My first focus of intervention, I decided, had to be with the parents, most of whom felt completely out of control and haunted daily by a burning sense of certainty that their child's unmanageable behavior was their fault. Dismantling incriminating beliefs requires that parents learn that ADHD is a *disorder*. This means that it is a specific problem with its own identity. Parents who are confronted with whining, acting out, sleep problems, and eating problems are encountering general challenges that impinge on all parents. ADHD does not affect all parents and *it has nothing to do with the consuming/consumed cycle of parenting*. So, although parents with ADHD children would rapidly fall into behaviors characteristic of the consumed/consuming cycle out of sheer desperation, *the cycle itself was not the cause of the disorder*.

The first step toward helping parents cope with ADHD is, obviously, to help parents recognize it.

This sounds easier than it is. For many, the first few years of the child's life have brought a disturbing but elusive array of problems: the child is easily distracted, easily upset, restless, emotionally volatile. These qualities leave parents feeling constantly overwhelmed and out of control, not to mention confused and guilty. Relatives and baby-sitters marvel at the endurance it takes "to put up with such a child." By the time the child is in preschool, notes from desperate teachers are already piling up in mailboxes.

To determine if this chapter is pertinent to your family, take a deep breath and answer the following questions:

- Has your child been described as "overly aggressive," "disturbed," "wild," "unmanageable," or "hyper- active"?
- Does your child have consistent difficulty in sleeping at night?
- Is your child unable to sit still for even short periods of time?
- Have you watched your child struggle to make friends but to little or no avail?
- Has your child ever asked you in hurt and bewilderment, "Why don't I have any friends?"
- Has a neighbor or relative forbidden your child to enter her house and/or play with her kids?
- Do the conflicting emotions of anger, love, hate, and frustration permeate your household?
- Do you frequently feel overwhelmed by your child's behavior, not knowing how to react to it or control it in constructive ways?

In the last 20 years, and especially in the past 10, there has been a growing awareness that children with behavior and learning problems are not all victims of a mental disorder or of bad parenting. Some children may have mental or parental problems; some are just normally active and exuberant; and *some are afflicted with a real, physical, and controllable illness—a "disability."*

In the early days of diagnosing this disorder, it was called "Minimal Brain Damage," "Minimal Brain Dysfunction" or "Hyperkinetic Syndrome" and/or "Hyperkinesis." The current diagnostic label, "Attention Deficit Hyperactive Disorder" (ADHD), is a more descriptive and more appropriate term in that it emphasizes that attention deficit disorders can exist *without* hyperactivity, or with varying degrees of hyperactivity.

As a pediatrician I am exposed to some very serious problems, both behavioral and physical in nature, that arise as a result of ADHD. In my daily buzzings from one room to another—between phone calls, diaper rashes, colic, formula changes, strep throats, bellyaches, wheezes, croup, and middle ear infections—I also encounter those frustrated and even desperate parents whose problem child needs action NOW.

Not all pediatricians are attuned to the diagnostic subtleties of ADHD. If you suspect your child is being affected by this disorder, I strongly recommend that you find a physician who is responsive to your perceptions and willing to work with you and your child on a consistent basis.

The most damaging myth surrounding ADHD is the assumption that a child's disruptive behavior results from a lack of parental authority and love. My personal experience leads me to believe that parental mismanagement rarely (if ever) is a primary source of this behavioral and learning disorder. It may add to the confusion and frustration, but it is *not* the prime cause.

Off-hand remarks from people saying that this is a disease of a particular socioeconomic class are just as disconcerting and misinformed as the accusation that we have created a disease for the drug. It is essential for you as parents to disregard the myth surrounding ADHD. It is not a personal indictment against you as parents and people; rather, *it is a treatable and controllable (though not yet curable) illness, like diabetes or seizure disorder.*

Clinical Picture

The German physician Heinrich Hoffman first described this condition over 100 years ago. Since that time, physicians and medical researchers have identified it as a chronic pediatric medical condition and developmental disability that occurs more frequently in boys (by a ratio of 4 or 5 to 1) and requires extensive management by parents and teachers and periodic re-evaluation by professionals.

ADHD is manifested by a symptom pattern of *hyperactivity, impulsiveness, distractibility,* and *excitability.* Aggressive and antisocial behavior, specific learning problems, and emotional instability are additional and common behavioral outgrowths of ADHD. It should be remembered that these behaviors reflect a *continuum of responses* that fluctuate in relation to environmental circumstances.

Diagnosis of ADHD is a complex task that involves identifying what it *is* as well as what it is *not.* For example, children with hearing or vision impairments may be suspected of having ADHD until their actual problems are uncovered. ADHD is easily confused with symptoms arising from a number of clinical disorders in addition to vision and hearing problems: specific learning disabilities (such as dyslexia), adjustment, mood, and anxiety disorders, petit mal seizures, and severe developmental disorders such as autism.

The typical child with ADHD is generally brought to professional attention early in his elementary school years. However, careful questioning usually reveals that symptoms have been present from early childhood. The clinical picture varies from the little boy who acts silly, immature, and performs below his level academically—to the child who acts like a tornado, is markedly aggressive and antisocial, and has severe learning problems.

The normal ebullience of childhood should not be confused with the special problems associated with ADHD. Frustrated adults reacting to a child who does not meet their standards can easily exaggerate the significance of occasional inner tension or restlessness. Above all, the characteristics of the disorder must be viewed from a developmental frame of reference—in other words, use common sense. The toddler is more restless and distractible than the school age child, and the school age child is certainly more distractible (by and large) than the adolescent.

Children with this disorder are often regarded as spoiled, ill-mannered, "odd," and uncoordinated. In actuality, they struggle with short attention spans and their actions are often lack direction, focus, or goal. Ongoing restless and impulsive behavior disrupts discipline in the home and classroom. Over and over again, the physician hears the same questions from parents who are concerned about *temper tantrums, persistent sleep problems, learning problems, aggressiveness, hyperactivity,* and *lack of friends.* Added to this list is the child's poor self-image ("I don't like myself"), which completes the painful cycle of failure, defeat, and isolation. (*See chart*)

Contrary to common misconceptions about children with this disorder, the ADHD child is neither brain-damaged, psychotic, nor mentally retarded. What these children do share are two very common problems that are both *developmental* in nature:

(1) social and sometimes physical immaturity, and
(2) the inability to select and appropriately respond to stimuli in the environment.

CHART

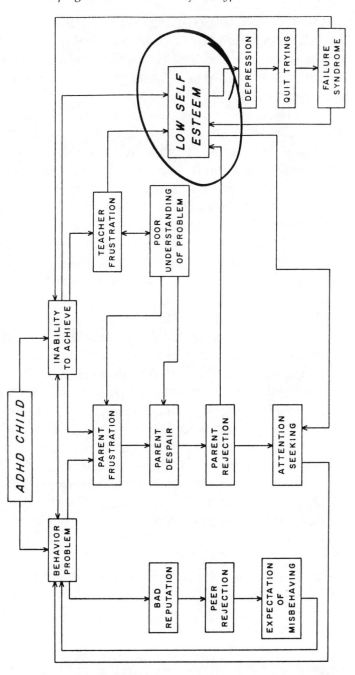

Once the concerned parent can begin to view this disorder through a "developmental looking-glass," so to speak, despair and futility are replaced with a larger perspective in which the immaturity will *eventually* give way to maturity.

To date, there is no simple cause or explanation for ADHD. For me, the best explanation is that we are dealing with a delayed maturation of the brain. This view is substantiated by the very obvious tendency for a significant number of children to improve as they grow older. Some children who have this disorder and go untreated do outgrow it without apparent problems. Indeed, there is not one of us who has not displayed some of the symptoms described above—yet, we are basically fine and well-adjusted adults (we hope!).

A formal definition of this disorder might be:
ADHD is a treatable illness that is characterized by involuntary behavior and/or learning problems in a child who may have a delayed maturation of the brain. The child's inability to control his span of concentration for a period of time long enough to assimilate and utilize incoming data results in uncontrolled emotional outbursts and emotional highs and lows—which in turn result in poor parent-child, poor teacher-child, and poor peer relationships. The resulting poor self-image perpetuates the cycle. (*Again, see chart*)

Let's take a closer look at the core characteristics of ADHD.

Hyperactivity

Symptoms of hyperactivity are usually present from an early age. Parents report that the child has always seemed to have an unusual amount of energy, has less need for sleep than his siblings, and has worn out shoes, clothes, bicycles, and probably one or both parents faster than the other children. Parents and teachers note that there is a pattern of continuous fidgeting: the child is unable to sit still for any length of time, talks a great deal, and cannot keep his hands to himself.

I wonder. Do these children actually have a *greater amount* of motor activity? Or do they have a *different type* of motor activity than the non-hyperactive child? I believe the difference is in *type*, not in amount.

Impulsiveness

Impulsiveness is demonstrated by quick, unpredictable movements without thought—behaviors such as jumping into the deep end of a swimming pool without knowing how to swim, running into the street in front of cars, darting out on ledges and high rooftops. In the verbal arena, the child often blurts out tactless and inappropriate statements.

Distractibility

This characteristic is more noticeable in the school-age child, but may also be reported by parents of pre-schoolers. Distractibility greatly disrupts this child's classwork and homework; he or she frequently daydreams, is easily distracted from projects by extraneous stimuli, and is unable to listen to a story or take part in table games for any length of time.

Excitability

Excitability in the ADHD child is expressed in temper tantrums and fights over trivial matters, and the tendency to become excessively active in stimulating situations. Disaster scenarios to be avoided are: *large groups of other children, department stores, parades, sporting events*, or even *family picnics.*

Antisocial Behavior

Aggressive, antisocial behaviors were originally considered inherent components of this particular disorder. However, careful clinical studies have revealed that there are only a small (but still significant) percentage of ADHD children who also manifest antisocial behavior when initially diagnosed. Since the percentage of these children who develop antisocial behaviors increases with age, it is very possible that the misbehavior develops as a reaction to the primary characteristics described above. Children who are unable to succeed in school, who are unable to develop satisfactory peer relationships, and who experience rejection at home and at school are likely to rebel against the values of family, school, and community.

Cognitive and Learning Disabilities

Virtually all clinical studies of children with this disorder have found that learning difficulties typically accompany it. However, the prevalence, nature, and educational expression of these difficulties are unclear and need more investigation. As mentioned, there is little doubt that the core symptoms can lead to a vicious cycle in which learning problems inevitably arise.

Other Emotional Symptoms

A wide variety of emotional problems and symptoms may be encountered in the ADHD child. In addition to antisocial behavior, the most significant of these are *depression* and *low self-esteem*. And like antisocial behavior, they are probably a secondary reaction to the continuing cycle of failure that the child encounters as a result of the core symptoms.

Maturational Changes in ADHD

It is worth emphasizing that this disorder changes with the age of the child. The diagnosis is most difficult to detect in infancy and the early preschool years. Mothers often report that their babies are unusually active, hyper-alert, and difficult to soothe. Irregularity of physiological functions—manifested by colic, sleep or eating disturbances, and frequent crying bouts —are also commonly reported. However, *it should be stressed that the presence of such problems are by no means an indication that the child is developing ADHD.*

Once a child begins to walk, other symptoms begin to appear. It is at this point that the hyperactive levels of behaviors coupled with attention difficulties become more noticeable. The typical child with ADHD seems to have a distinct lack of a sense of danger; he or she moves from one activity to another very rapidly, and is relatively impervious to the disciplinary measures parents previously found effective with their other children.

It is when the ADHD child reaches the school system that the diagnosis is most often and most easily made. Behaviors that were disturbing but tolerable in the home are not so easily tolerated in the classroom. Academic problems increase with the passage of time, and antisocial behaviors become more prevalent.

By the onset of adolescence, educational retardation, antisocial behavior, depression, and low self-esteem are the most common presenting problems. But since the classic ADHD symptoms of hyperactivity, distractibility, impulsiveness, and excitability have probably lessened with the age of the child, these secondary problems during adolescence often obscure the diagnosis. A careful developmental history usually reveals the earlier symptoms of ADHD.

The clinical picture of this child as an adult remains unclear. To date, there are no published longitudinal studies of this disorder that follow the child's progress into adolescence and beyond. I have followed a number of my own patients into young adulthood, however, and my experience leads me to believe that they have as good a chance of surviving society's pressures (if they have been treated) as do other young adults. Indeed, they should be well able to adjust to the challenges and stresses that commonly confront all of us, if medical treatment and supportive therapy are continued.

Screening Your Child

Several years ago I realized that there had to be a better way to deal with the pressures of ADHD than offering halfway answers in the office corridors and prescribing medication as the sole solution. I decided that a good screening test, manned by a competent and caring pediatrician, would save everyone involved time and grief.

I felt strongly that the two best resources for identifying the child with this disorder were the parents and the child's teachers. Through many preliminary studies comparing ADHD children with children who had no behavior or learning problems (appropriately matched in age and socioeconomic background), behavior evaluation forms for parents and teachers evolved (*Appendices 1 and 2; Appendix 3 lists additional behavior rating scales*). The score derived from this form is but one of the tools that can be made available to the physician and the parents to aid in the diagnosis of the child's problem. It should be noted that careful history-taking and the elimination of organic brain damage as a possible cause are very important starting points in the process of diagnosis.

In addition to helping parents identify the problem, this behavior form can also be very useful in superseding the unbidden diagnoses of neighbors, relatives, and friends. Very often, the form simply leads to counseling regarding normal behavior problems. Most importantly, it is the stimulus for initiating help—for finding a solution as well as for identifying this specific problem. *The score, the child's history, and the school's evaluation should not be disregarded or taken lightly just because the mother has not had a nervous breakdown yet!*

The physical examination of children with ADHD is usually completely normal. The only time I have found evidence of a problem occurs when the child is kept waiting in a small examining room with his mother. It is not surprising to find the mother hiding behind the trash can and the child hanging from a rafter! I'm not so sure that this behavior would be a significant finding, however!

Brain wave tests have been proven to be inconclusive in relation to ADHD. There simply is no consistent brain wave pattern that is specifically characteristic of the disorder. As far as psychometric testing is concerned, research has shown a disappointing lack of relationship between this disorder and the psychological tests and psychologists' ratings. From a practical point of view, the child who has this disorder is certainly not going to perform well in the psychologist's office under a battery of tests (which cost somewhere between $200 and $500) that determine how poorly he can concentrate and how easily he can become frustrated and explosive!

Treatment

Today, fortunately, we can present a more unified approach to this problem based on sound information and sympathetic understanding.

Identifying the child with the behavior and/or learning problems associated with ADHD gives us a welcome direction. At this point, many options for intervention become available:

1. No medication; counseling for normal behavior problems
2. No medication; educational therapy alone
3. Medication alone
4. Medication and educational therapy
5. Medication and counseling by the consulting physician
6. Psychological testing and then medication as needed
7. Psychological testing, family counseling, and no medication
8. Psychiatric counseling for the more severe problems.

It may be necessary to use any combination of these, or all of them together. The most important point is to begin treatment *early*. Timely intervention prevents or reduces secondary emotional problems, helps the entire family function better, decreases the pattern of failure for the child in school, and lessens the child's chances of developing poor self-esteem syndrome.

Drug Therapy

My first choice of therapy in treating ADHD children is drug therapy, and my drug of choice is Ritalin. Since there is always a possibility that the drug alone may not work, I will combine the drug with counseling or educational therapy when indicated.

Medication is valuable in the overall care of ADHD children by reducing their levels of excitability and impulsiveness and by increasing their attention spans. Strangely enough, Ritalin (and other drugs prescribed for this disorder) is a stimulant rather than a sedative. Stimulant medication enchances communication between nerve cells and activates certain areas of the brain that control attention, arousal and inhibitory processes.

The primary object of medication is not to calm the child, as one might think. Rather, it is to improve brain functioning so that the child can select from his environment the stimuli that will allow him to behave in a manner appropriate for a particular situation. (Recent research reveals that the medication may, in fact, stimulate a particular enzyme in the brain; one can speculate that this enzyme, if it can be identified, might become the focus of new treatment.) This "normalizing" action of the medication not only allows the child to be less hyperactive, less belligerent, and better able to follow directions, but it also lengthens the attention span, decreases the levels of distractibility, and may even improve coordination.

Initially the medication should be prescribed in very small doses. Some physicians have the child take it twice a day in order to handle the problem during school hours. I feel that the problem *usually* exists on a 24-hour basis and therefore most often recommend that it be taken three times a day. When the problem is limited to attention deficit and learning problems, without the qualities of impulsiveness and excitability, then it can be taken only twice a day.

In the beginning I suggest that the medication be taken only five days out of the week. The five-day-week regimen is useful because it gives parents a source of comparison and helps them to be more objective in viewing some of the drug-related changes, which initially may be very subtle. The parents remain in constant contact with the physician with reports about the child's behavior. Dosage changes are often necessary until the optimum dosage has been established, at which point the child begins to take the medication on a daily basis.

I strongly recommend that teachers be informed when a child begins taking medication because their observations are equally important in terms of dosage control. Apprising teachers also makes them aware that the problem is being faced, and they then may join in your "team" as your dedicated partners along with your physician.

Once the drug therapy is begun, I recommend 15-minute office visits with the child and parent every two to three months so that follow-up can be maintained. With regard to feedback from teachers, written or phone reports are sufficient. Initially, these reports can be given every two weeks. Once the dosage has been established and the symptoms have improved or abated, the length of time between reports can be lengthened to every three or four months.

Too often, parents will accept undesired behavioral changes that are completely unnecessary. The same dosage for one year or longer may be doing more harm than good. It is important that parents understand what to look for when a regression in behavior occurs, so that if there is a need for dosage change, the physician can be consulted immediately. Needless to say, *parents should never increase medication on their own.*

"What About Drug Addiction?"

The suggestion that the administration of this medication can lay the foundation for future drug addiction is unfounded. Ritalin does not create a pattern or predisposition in the child to turn to drugs in order to handle unpleasant feelings and situations. As a matter of fact, many children resent the idea of having to take medication in order to function within their environment in an approved manner. I believe that the *untreated* youngster, who has had years of frustration and humiliation in the classroom, is a much more likely candidate for drug involvement.

"What About Side-Effects?"

Because every individual reacts in his or her own unique way to a drug, any untoward effects stop once the medication has been discontinued. There are side-effects to the stimulant medication, as there as with any drug. Some of the more common complaints, such as headaches or heart pain (in younger children, this usually means rapid heartbeat), come with initial medication or dosage changes and last only a day or two. Insomnia is usually not a new side-effect for children with this disorder. Because *stimulant* medication is being used, parents often assume that a sleep problem will inevitably occur. Many children with ADHD have had sleep problems from day one anyway! They are generally children who do not require a lot of sleep (perhaps like one or both of their parents), which is also a very individual requirement. If a real change in the child's sleep pattern does occur, however, the afternoon dose can be given earlier.

In general, there should be no loss of appetite due to

the drug, and if there is, the loss is probably psychological in nature. Five of the 375 children I have on stimulant medication are obese—and not one has lost an ounce because of it! So while a small percentage of children may show a noticeable decrease in appetite, I have not found it to be a disturbing side-effect.

A significant amount of research over the past two decades has shown that stimulant medication for children with ADHD enhances a wide variety of cognitive and behavioral processes.[1] In my many years of prescribing Ritalin for ADHD, I have found that there is striking and at times even unbelievable improvement in both the child's behavior and academic performance. Naturally, these improvements result in enhanced self-esteem and greater acceptance by classmates, teachers, and family. The end result, hopefully, is that you will finally have a child who is able to function well within his or her environment—and even enjoy it in the process! While no guarantees are possible, there is a realistic basis for hope if you seek help from your pediatrician.

"What About Those Newspaper Reports?"

In the past few years, sensationalistic journalism has fostered an avalanche of misinformation about stimulant medication that has frightened parents and teachers alike. Disconcerting headlines such as "Pills to Quiet Kids Suppress Growth" have appeared in the press, causing much unwarranted distress. For example, a study by one physician in an apparently well-written article attempted to distort this issue by sensationally reporting that children treated on a longterm basis with stimulant medication grew one-eighth of an inch less

---

[1] For a review of the research in this area, see the following two sources:

Barkley, R. (1977). A review of stimulant drug research with hyperactive children. *Journal of Child Psychology and Psychiatry, 18*, 137-165.

Donnelly, M., & Rapoport, J. (1985). Attention deficit disorders. In J. Weiner (Ed.), *Diagnosis and Psychopharmacology of Childhood and Adolescent Disorders* (pp.178-198). New York: Wiley.

each year than children of the same age who were not taking medication. His results have not been duplicated in other studies—and without scientific replication, his findings are not valid.

It should be comforting to know that researchers have replicated studies showing that the actual side-effects accruing from stimulant medications are very mild relative to other kinds of medications. You can see for yourself.[2] To claim that these pills are being used "to keep kids quiet" is paradoxical at best and ignorant at worst: it is *stimulant* medication that makes the brain function *more effectively*; it is not one bit sedating in nature! Unfortunately, such misdirected articles can have worse effects than poor therapy or no therapy at all. Whenever you read or hear anything in the media that distresses you concerning your family's health, place an immediate call to your physician and check out the information.

The Combination Plate

The eight- or nine-year-old child who has had ADHD for a number of years now has more than just a "learning problem": he or she also has a problem in *how to learn*. In these cases I strongly recommend that drug therapy be combined with educational therapy. The educational therapist teaches not just subject matter (like a tutor does) but *learning processes*. The ADHD child learns how to learn in relation to his or her own attentional and perceptual disabilities in an optimal environment that fosters self-motivation. No less importantly, the educational therapist gives us a fourth partner in helping to evaluate the medication.

---

[2] Barkley, R. (1990). *Attention Deficit Hyperactivity Disorder: A Handbook for Diagnosis and Treatment.* New York: Guilford Press.

Barkley, R., McMurray, M., Edelbrock, C., and Robbins, K. (1990). Side-effects of methylphenidate in children with attention deficit hyperactivity disorder: a systematic, placebo-controlled evaluation. *Pediatrics, 86*, 184-192.

What is the role of mental health professionals in helping the ADHD child and his or her family? In general I view their primary role as one of consultants working with the physician when one or more combinations of other forms of therapy has failed to raise the functioning level of the child to its optimum. However, there are some children who, by the time they come to me, have real emotional sequelae as a result of the ADHD. When that is the case, I recommend that the medication and educational therapy be further supplemented by regular therapy sessions with a counselor, therapist, psychologist, or psychiatrist. Needless to say, if we are dealing with a child who is also psychotic, or with troubled parents who are creating an unstable environment for their child, then intervention by a mental health professional should be sought immediately. In my experience, there is a greater need for consultation from these professionals when children are past the age of seven or eight—probably because they and their parents have suffered more emotionally as a result of the primary problem of ADHD.

Other Theories and Tidbits

Our discussion of ADHD would not be complete without mentioning the potpourri of additional causes and solutions that have received attention: hypoglycemia, the "wild chocolate syndrome" (additional causes), and megavitamins, caffeine, and Feingold's diet (additional solutions).

There is little supporting evidence linking ADHD with hypoglycemia. Regarding the "wild chocolate syndrome," there is plenty of "home-grown" proof that some children become hyperactive after indulging in candy, particularly chocolate. Many teachers can attest to this fact following Halloween! Parents often find that reducing or eliminating sugar from their children's diets does indeed lessen the hyperactive thrust of their behavior. (Keep in mind that this sugar-induced hyperactivity *does not* mean that these children, who have an inborn sensitivity to sweets, will also develop ADHD.)

In regard to taking megavitamins as a means of lessening hyperactive behavior, I have strong feelings that the human body can absorb only the vitamins it can make use of, and then no more. I seriously doubt that megavitamins can ameliorate in any way the symptoms of the ADHD child.

Concerning caffeine, if you have very strong feelings against the stimulant medications that are now available, giving coffee as an alternative is certainly worth trying. However, there is very little research in the medical literature on this topic. By all means, consult your physician before creating your own caffeine remedy.

Twelve years ago Dr. Ben Feingold advocated a dietary solution of eliminating all foods with artificial flavoring. The medical validity of this diet is still in limbo because there are no reported controlled studies. Ten years ago, I subjected ten of my ADHD patients between the ages of 6 and 11 to the diet. The results of this experience were near disaster, because the entire family had to go through hell in trying to maintain it. However, if your family is opposed to medication because of religious beliefs, or there is a drug sensitive condition, this *may be* the answer. My feeling is that, if stimulant medication can accomplish the same beneficial results and not break up a relatively happy family by necessitating a police state at home, using the medication is easier than the diet!

Suggestions to Parents

Ideally, the first stage of change in a positive direction takes place in your attitude and outlook. When you as a parent understand that your child has a treatable illness caused by a delayed maturation of the brain— and that he or she is acting *involuntarily* instead of personally attacking you—you will be more willing and able to apply firm and consistent discipline without the added burden of anger.

The second stage of change is quite practical in nature: *Avoid, divide, and conquer!* Avoid shopping trips and multi-activity days. Activities should be kept brief and should not exceed your child's capability for sustained attention. Instruction should be unambiguous and promptly enforced. When early signs of impending temper tantrums surface, take immediate steps to remove your child from the situation and offer him or her an alternative. If an explosion does occur, there is nothing to do but wait it out, making sure that no one is harmed and that your child does not gain his or her ends by such tyranny. This is basically the same advice I would offer a parent whose "normal" child is indulging in temper tantrums.

As your child gets older and/or gains more self-control, you can initiate multi-activity experiences—but *very slowly*. Time is like money: when invested correctly, you net a substantial return.

A Final Word

Don't panic and don't wring your hands in despair. You are dedicated and courageous parents who are trying to create a normal environment for your child under very challenging conditions. Find out that you are not alone by contacting the newly formed national resource organization for parents called "CHADD," Children with Attention Deficit Disorders (1859 N. Pine Island Rd., Suite 185, Plantation, FL 33322, 305/384-6869).

Remember—all of the love, caring, and time will not be enough if there is no identification of the problem. If you are reading this, you are seeking answers. And that is the first step toward solving the problem.

ASK FOR HELP.
YOU AND YOUR CHILD DESERVE ALL THE
SUPPORT YOU CAN GET.

Appendix 1 🍎

PARENT RATING
BEHAVIOR FORMS

Child's Name_____ Age___ Sex___ Date _____

1.	Unusually hyperactive	HOME	SCHOOL	BOTH	NO
2.	Jumps from one activity to another			YES	NO
3.	Short attention span			YES	NO
4.	Fidgets	SOMETIMES	CONSTANT		NO
5.	Is unpredictable, unmanageable			YES	NO
6.	Irritable			YES	NO
7.	Overly sensitive			YES	NO
8.	Quick tempered, explosive			YES	NO
9.	Panics easily			YES	NO
10.	Tolerance for failure and frustration is low			YES	NO
11.	Emotionally high strung			YES	NO
12.	Becomes anxious or upset when told ahead of time about an outing or appointment			YES	NO
13.	Exceptionally clumsy			YES	NO
14.	Poor coordination			YES	NO
15.	Eyes and hands don't seem to function together			YES	NO
16.	Has trouble buttoning			YES	NO
17.	Has trouble drawing, writing			YES	NO
18.	Was slow learning to walk			YES	NO
19.	Trouble with bicycle			YES	NO
20.	Trouble with catching ball			YES	NO
21.	Speech development has been slow			YES	NO
22.	Speech is not clear			YES	NO

23. Reacts adversely to changes in routine   YES   NO
24. Can't seem to keep from touching everything
and everyone around him   YES   NO
25. No learning in school although seems "bright"   YES   NO
26. Child is lazy—not "trying" to do well in school   YES   NO
27. Daydreams while doing homework   YES   NO
28. Knows work orally at home—gets to school
and has to write it down—fails miserably   YES   NO

Appendix 2 🍒

SCHOOL EVALUATION
(To be filled out by child's teacher)

Child's Name _____ Teacher's Name _____

This child...	Never	Almost Never	Some Times	Almost Always	Always
1. Is a behavioral problem in class	___	___	___	___	___
2. Is quiet and withdrawn— a loner	___	___	___	___	___
3. Is unable to follow directions	___	___	___	___	___
4. Finds it hard to play with peers	___	___	___	___	___
5. Seems to touch everything and everyone around him	___	___	___	___	___
6. Has a short attention span	___	___	___	___	___
7. Fidgets	___	___	___	___	___

This child...	Never	Almost Never	Some Times	Almost Always	Always
8. Is unable to focus attention on any particular activity	___	___	___	___	___
9. Is quick-tempered, explosive	___	___	___	___	___
10. Has a low tolerance for failure and frustration	___	___	___	___	___
11. Can't seem to get eyes and hands to function together	___	___	___	___	___
12. Is exceptionally clumsy	___	___	___	___	___
13. Has poor coordination	___	___	___	___	___
14. Reacts adversely to changes in routine	___	___	___	___	___
15. Is slow or not clear in speech development	___	___	___	___	___

Appendix 3 ❦

Additional Behavior Rating Scales

For Parents

1. *THE ANSER PARENT QUESTIONNAIRE*
Levine, M.D. (1980). *The Anser System.* Cambridge, Mass.: Educators Publishing Service.

2. *ATTENTION DEFICIT DISORDERS EVALUATION SCALE*
McCarney, S.B. (1989). *The Attention Deficit Disorders Evaluation Scale, Home Version, Technical Manual.* Columbia, Mo.: Hawthorne Educational Services.

3. *CONNERS PARENT RATING SCALE—REVISED*
   Goyette, C.H., Conners, C.K., & Ulrich, R.F. (1978). Normative data on the revised Conners Parent and Teacher Rating Scales. *Journal of Abnormal Child Psychology, 6*, 221.

4. *YALE CHILDREN'S INVENTORY*
   Shaywitz, S.E., Schnell, C., Shaywitz, B.A., et al. (1986). Yale Children's Inventory (YCI): An instrument to assess children with attentional deficits and learning disabilities—scale development and psychometric properties. *Journal of Abnormal Child Psychology, 14*, 347.

For Teachers

1. *ADD-H: COMPREHENSIVE TEACHER RATING SCALE*
   Ullman, R.K., Sleator, E.K., & Sprague, R.L. (1984). A new rating scale for diagnosis and monitoring of ADD children. *Psychopharmacological Bulletin, 20*, 160.

2. *ANSER TEACHER QUESTIONNAIRE*
   Levine, M.D. (1980). *The Anser System.* Cambridge, Mass.: Educators Publishing Service.

3. *ATTENTION DEFICIT DISORDERS EVALUATION SCALE*
   McCarney, S.B. (1989). *The Attention Deficit Disorders Evaluation Scale, School Version, Technical Manual.* Columbia, Mo.: Hawthorne Educational Services.

4. *CONNERS TEACHER RATING SCALE—REVISED*
   Goyette, C.H., Conners, C.K., & Ulrich, R.F. (1978). Normative data on the revised Conners Parent and Teacher Rating Scales. *Journal of Abnormal Child Psychology, 6,* 221.

5. *TEACHER'S REPORT FORM*
   Edelbrock, C., & Achenback, T.M. (1984). The teacher version of the Child Behavioral Profile: l. Boys aged 6-11. *Journal of Consulting and Clinical Psychology, 52,* 207.